Margaret Richard

BODY ELECTRIC

Strong, Toned, and Sexy

in Just 3 Hours a Week

New York   Chicago   San Francisco   Lisbon   London   Madrid   Mexico City
Milan   New Delhi   San Juan   Seoul   Singapore   Sydney   Toronto

The McGraw·Hill Companies

Library of Congress Cataloging-in-Publication Data

Richard, Margaret.
    Body electric : strong, toned, and sexy in just three hours a week / Margaret
Richard.
      p.   cm.
      Includes index.
      ISBN 978-0-07-154480-1 (alk. paper)
      1. Physical fitness.   2. Exercise.   3. Muscle strength.   I. Title.

RA781.R525 2008
613.7—dc22   2007039656

1 2 3 4 5 6 7 8 9 10 11 12 13 14 15 16 17 18 19 20 21   WCT/WCT   0 9 8

ISBN 978-0-07-154480-1
MHID   0-07-154480-1

Interior photography by Jon Abeyta

McGraw-Hill books are available at special quantity discounts to use as premiums and
sales promotions or for use in corporate training programs. To contact a representative,
please visit the Contact Us pages at www.mhprofessional.com.

This book is printed on acid-free paper.

This book is dedicated to

my children, Todd and Brooke,

and my husband, Jack,

who give me the opportunity

to love unconditionally.

Contents

PART 1
Define Your Potential with Strength—Not Age

PART 2

The Dynamic Exercises

Acknowledgments

I am deeply grateful for the many people and life experiences that helped to shape this book. I wouldn't change a thing.

In chronological order:

Love and gratitude to my mother and late father, May and Saul Sokal, for my education and creative spirit; my relatives, the Green and Ascarelli families, who provided nurturance during my early years; the late Dorothy Lear, principal of the Lear School, for her compassion, understanding, and respect; my high school friend Beverly Culmo, who affectionately called me Chiquita; Barry Richard, for twenty married years and our two cherished children; and the Richard family, who counted me among their own.

It was a privilege to share that first thrilling wave of success with my Tallahassee friends and the Body Electric studio instructors, including Beth Switzer, for her talent and charisma; Karen Meyers and Ellyn Alkon, who were there from the beginning; and Patrick Keating, for inviting me to produce "Body Electric" at WFSU-TV, Florida State University's PBS station. Much appreciation and affection to the many Body Electric dancers who contributed to the studio and television shows in Tallahassee, most notably Kathy Doolin, Mary Barley, Benisa Forté, Kim Jogensen, Natalie Sherako, Alan David, Cathy Kelly, Jorge Perez, Missy Gracey, Sherma Dillard, Guy Davis, Kenya Morris, Joe Hodges, Jules Bevis, Patty McAlpine, LaDonna Hartman, Jill Harper, and the late Javose Burnett. I could always count on my dear friends Beth Mueller, Berneice Cox, and especially Jane Marks to infuse true delight into our shared experiences.

Thanks to the dancers who unselfishly worked until 4 A.M. to produce our very first video, *Body Shaping*, set at Studebaker's Nightclub in Tallahassee; and Nancy Kunkle and others who created overwhelming success in our Gainesville studio.

I am deeply grateful to Dan Boroto, Ph.D., for his wise counsel and for teaching me that there are no failures, only opportunities to succeed; and to my sister-friends—Priscilla Quinones, Jane Marks, Susan Turner, Ann Gabor, Lois Randall, Candy Klieman, Anne Armel, and Susan Gamburg—whose love, devotion, and support made everything possible.

I treasure my cousins Marlene Cain, Susan Davis, and Julie Sokal-Harris, the "honey" Kenny Cain, and Nana and John Greller, who continue to express love, kindness, and support; thanks go to Aunt Susan and Uncle Dennis Richard, for embracing Todd and Brooke and sharing the most precious of gifts.

Sincere appreciation to the Buffalo crew, who picked up the ball and made it possible to continue production of the "Body Electric" show, most notably Don Boswell and Jim Dimino at WNED-TV; Cathy Stoldt, hair and makeup artist and production assistant, for her dedication, keen eye, and good-natured spirit; dancers including Kathy Privatera, Stephanie McDonell, Rebecca Haslinger, Leslie Just, and Beverly Ann Shipe; Robyn Zimmer, Sharron Camp-Reed, and dear Heidi Billittier, my Buffalo "sisters," who provided much love and support during our Orchard Park "backyard" productions; all of the beautiful women and my treasured octogenarian friend, Don Mueller, who faithfully attend my classes at the YMCA; my husband, Jack Fox, for taking time away from his law practice to run the cameras and assist in the production and editing of the "Body Electric" shows; my assistant Tracy Glenn for never missing a beat at the office; and "Tall Girls" Pam and Deb, for always hitting the mark with graphic design.

Kudos and appreciation to my agent, Linda Konner, for patiently walking me through the entire book-writing process; John Abeyta assisted by Robert John, for always making me smile and never taking a bad photo; my talented editor at McGraw-Hill, Deb Brody, whose advice was always right-on—especially regarding my corny comments; and contributors to this book: Karen Roberts, M.S.N., ARNP-C; Joan Price; John O. Wycoff, D.O.; and Michel D. Storch, M.D., F.A.C.S. Thank you to Larry Muscoreil, general manager of the Orchard Park Borders Superstore, and the folks at the café, Rose, Jennelle, James, and Stephanie, who prepared the best iced coffee and made me feel welcome during the many hours spent writing this book.

I am forever indebted to the "Body Electric" PBS television viewers, "the friends," who embrace me as I embrace them. Over twenty-plus years we have shared a special bond that continues to grow stronger.

Love to my precious mother-in-law, Leona Fox, and our large circle of relatives, friends, and neighbors in the Buffalo area. By the way, don't believe everything you hear about Buffalo weather—the winters are poetically beautiful.

Siber, my handsome Siberian husky, gives me special joy—I never thought I would be such a dog person.

My dearest Brooke and Todd are my life's greatest accomplishments. I cherish being their mom; I also love and adore my son-in-law, David Gerzof, my daughter's true love.

Jack, you once asked me where I find my "grace," and my answer is that I find it each day with you.

Define Your Potential with Strength—Not Age

PART 1

CHAPTER 1

Lighting the Body Electric Spark

Some things never get old. You certainly don't tire of vibrant health, youthful energy, radiant good looks, and the strength to live your life any way you please. Unfortunately, our bodies *do* get old—but old doesn't have to mean weak and flabby. The Body Electric program offers this promise: with regular participation you will continue to realize stronger muscles, denser bones, better balance, increased energy—and that's just the beginning. You will walk taller, reach lower, lift heavier, and have a quality of life that is defined by the things you *can* do rather than those you can't.

Whether you are forty or eighty, strength and muscle mass *can* be increased. The resistance-type exercises offered in this program serve to counteract many age-related conditions, such as weakened muscles, osteoporosis, stiff joints, and the inevitable weight gain in all the wrong places (are there any right places?).

The Body Electric Story

My passion for fitness, form, and graceful movement got its start when I began dancing as a young girl. At the age of eight, I auditioned for the theater legends Richard Rodgers and Oscar Hammerstein and was cast in the role of the plantation owner's daughter in the 1956 Broadway revival of *South Pacific*. I haven't stopped moving since!

My great fortune was that doing what I loved, studying ballet, prepared me for a career—and unexpected success—in fitness. My first foray into teaching dance exercise and fitness was in 1979, after giving birth to my second child. I was living in Tallahassee, Florida, and invited about forty-five friends and acquaintances to attend my first class. We were a ragtag crew dressed in leotards, bathing suits, and bare feet, but we knew we were on to something good—very good.

The promise of renewed strength, vigor, and muscle tone was not a hard sell. The spark was lit, and the Body Electric program took off like wildfire. Our intense enthusiasm did not go unnoticed. A local cable television station offered to produce a daily exercise show at 6 P.M., opposite the news. That show led to one produced by the PBS station at Florida State University. As they say, the rest is history.

I've now been teaching the Body Electric program for nearly thirty years, and for more than twenty of those years, I've been appearing daily on PBS television. I am dedicated to helping you, my fellow baby boomer, preserve your youthfulness by delaying the negative effects of aging. We want to live fully into old age, not just survive, and this book will show you how.

Fanning the Flames of Motivation

You're likely reading this book because you either want to start an exercise program or want to improve or shake up the exercise routine that you're currently doing. Just by reading this paragraph, you've taken the first, sometimes most difficult, and certainly one of the most important steps to being a dedicated exerciser, and that is being motivated.

I can't give you the exact formula for motivation, because motivation has to be based on uniquely personal values. What motivates you may not be the same as what motivates me, or your sister, or your next-door neighbor. Furthermore, fitness is a lifelong pursuit that is accomplished one workout at a time. As you exercise with the Body Electric program, keep in mind that even small successes will lead to quantum improvements in

Cathy's Story

I met Cathy, age sixty-two, shortly after I began teaching classes at the Orchard Park YMCA. Cathy was running laps around the track; I was enjoying a brisk walk. I admired Cathy's effortless running style and was surprised later to learn that she suffers from rheumatoid arthritis. Cathy was a new convert to the Body Electric program but had been an avid exerciser for years. "I was totally impressed with the class from the very beginning," she says. "Margaret strengthens and tones each muscle group in so many different ways. The degree of intensity is determined by your choice of weights used, so while I am probably thirty years older than many women in the class, I am able to strengthen each muscle group at my own rate. I have increased the weights over time to continue to work to my maximum.

"I joined Margaret's class shortly after being treated for a thyroid condition and was pretty well wiped out. Being part of the class gives me an overall feeling of well-being. I am grateful for the health that I have and want to preserve it."

Cathy and her husband, Tony, raised five children, and despite a crazy schedule, she always made exercise a priority for the whole family. "Our family did everything together—skiing, biking, swimming, tennis, canoeing, golfing, and hiking parts of the Appalachian Trail," Cathy says. She also ran several half-marathons. "I found that if I stayed organized, I could eliminate the frazzle part of our daily life."

your health and well-being. Your investments of time and energy will ultimately pay off in ways you can't even imagine.

For sure, there will be times when your muscle development seems to plateau or your motivation stalls—it happens to all of us. Your fitness and energy levels may fluctuate from day to day, for a variety of reasons. You may not have had enough to eat the day before, so your energy is flagging, or you may have had too much to eat or drink the night before, and your body is recovering. Lack of sleep will definitely rob you of precious energy. Give your motivation a jump-start by keeping

Over the years, though, Cathy encountered her share of medical problems. One of the lowest points was a skiing accident in Utah. "My husband and I were at the top of a very icy mountain and started to sidestep down. It was solid ice and we were above the tree line. I slipped and slid about eight hundred feet before crashing into a tree. Some of my ski equipment went over a cliff—thankfully, without me. My lower left leg was badly broken as I bounced down the ice." Cathy was flown to a trauma center, where she had a rod surgically implanted. This was followed by months of recovery spent in bed, after which she had to use a wheelchair and then crutches.

Looking back, Cathy realizes that she would have been even better at her athletic activities if she had participated in the Body Electric program sooner. As active as she was, she did no specific strength training and no exercises that targeted the muscles of her upper body. "Strengthening each muscle group would have provided a tremendous benefit," she says. "So many programs fell short of what I would have liked to accomplish, but Body Electric is appropriate for everyone, at every level."

Cathy's upbeat personality and strong determination are readily apparent. She continues to regularly attend my classes at the Y and even reports a surprise fitness bonus: increased upper-body strength has improved her golf swing! Although Cathy's ability to overcome medical challenges shows great will and determination, the beauty of Cathy's story is her commitment to fitness and the inherent joy it brings her. Cathy is empowered and strong—and her spirit shines! Plus, she appears as strong as anyone thirty years younger.

your eye on the prize: lifelong health and fitness that builds with discipline and consistency. You can better understand the path progress takes by using the analogy of a child's growth: it is not apparent from day to day; however, over time there are significant changes.

I experience each workout as a life-affirming infusion of health and energy. Needless to say, my relationship with fitness is deeply ingrained and totally positive. But there is no free ride. You have to work to earn every gain, and you have to stay motivated and believe that what you are doing is important.

Being purpose-driven helps you accomplish your goals. How you think probably has more to do with your ability to maintain fitness than anything else. If you're not completely dedicated to the idea, no fitness plan in the world will work. After all, it's much easier to practice self-discipline when you are clear about your goals.

> "How we spend our days is, of course, how we spend our lives."
>
> —ANNIE DILLARD

Studies have shown that believing in the exercise you're doing may actually make it more effective. People who think they're getting a good workout obtain more benefits than those who perform the exact same activities but don't think what they are doing is exercise, according to a study by Harvard researcher Dr. Ellen Langer and her student Alia J. Crum published in *Psychological Science*. They wrote, "Whether the change in physiological health was brought about directly or indirectly, it is clear that health is significantly affected by mind-set."

Never sell yourself short. Success or failure is not a matter of luck, and those who succeed are ultimately able to withstand the anxiety that often accompanies change. Don't be afraid to go out on a limb and dance on the "skinny branches"! You will accomplish your goals with more integrity and live a more meaningful and satisfying existence.

Your Corporate Body

Would you choose to be the head of a corporation? Actually, you already are the chief executive officer of your body. As CEO, you are ultimately responsible for the success or failure of your "company." The buck stops with you! As the corporate "head"—literally—your most important task is to make sure that all of your company's day-to-day activities remain committed to the grander vision. You are the one person who oversees all the links to make sure they are working toward the common goal; the decisions you make critically affect the fate of your company. So, before you eat that next double-dip ice-cream cone, ask yourself how this action will fly with corporate.

State Your Mission

We know the effect that gravity can have on our bodies, and it can be daunting! Exercise with resistance tightens and tones the muscles and strengthens the bones; aerobic exercise reduces body fat. Add a nutritious, low-fat diet, stretching exercises for flexibility, and the right amount of rest and relaxation, and you have the perfect antigravity prescription.

But let's get real! That formula works only if you are able to say yes to the long-term commitment. Good executives study long-term, short-term, and intermediate goals and weigh their implications. Successful companies have a well-defined mission statement that outlines the company's purpose, values, and goals for the future. It expresses strategies for success that are inspirational and relevant.

As the head of your corporate body, give thought to your most compelling vision, and write a mission statement as a game plan to realize that vision. The best mission statement is only a few concise sentences in length. For example, here is mine:

1. My mission: to live my life with vibrancy, strength, and purpose. I wish to always remain grateful for my talents and my ability to use them to empower others.
2. My fitness strategy:
   a. *Muscle and bone strengthening:* continue to challenge my muscles as I teach three one-hour muscle-toning classes per week.

b. *Aerobic exercise:* walk briskly for thirty to forty-five minutes at least five days each week.

c. *Stretching:* perform a muscle-specific stretch at the end of each exercise, as well as a five-minute stretch at the conclusion of each muscle-toning and aerobic workout.

d. *Nutrition:* fine-tune my nutrition by reading nutritional updates and meeting with a dietitian periodically.

e. *Rest and relaxation:* learn to meditate.

3. My values: continue to benefit from new insights and divergent points of view. Good health and loving relationships with family and friends are treasures I will never take for granted.

Now write your own, following this format:

1. What are your personal goals?

_____

_____

_____

2. How do you plan to meet these goals? (Your strategy should capitalize on your actual strengths.)

_____

_____

_____

3. Comment on your values and moral compass. (As the CEO of your "corporate body," you are the only person who can make things work.)

_____

_____

_____

Value Your Flaws:
The Philosophy of Wabi Sabi

Wabi sabi is the ancient Japanese philosophy that teaches us to appreciate the beauty inherent in things that are naturally flawed, uniquely imperfect, and purely simple. Ancient Greek standards defined beauty as being flawless. This unattainable standard of perfection continues to breed discontent and feelings of inadequacy in our modern Western culture. In stark contrast, Asian culture embraces a more forgiving aesthetic that embraces our flaws and organic nature, just as we are.

In the spirit of wabi sabi, I encourage you to celebrate your uniqueness with exercise and nutrition programs that are a custom fit for you. Take time each day to create beauty in yourself and at the same time value imperfection. The Body Electric program offers exercise variations for each muscle group with positions standing, sitting, and lying on the floor. Try something new. Vary your workouts.

We boomers want a fitness program that respects our vibrancy while remaining convenient, affordable, effective, and enjoyable—with no negative side effects. That's a tall order, but the Body Electric program *will* deliver. With just one Body Electric thirty- to sixty-minute exercise session every three days, you will develop stronger muscles, denser bones, and a more fit body. No need to choose between firm arms or a tight butt. You can have it all.

This fitness program is like no other. I have not reinvented the wheel—just provided a different spin. Now let's begin your journey to health and fitness!

> "The Japanese view of life embraced a simple aesthetic that grew stronger as inessentials were eliminated and trimmed away."
>
> —TADAO ANDO, ARCHITECT

CHAPTER 2

Suiting Up

The Body Electric Fitness Formula

Are you aware of feeling more alive under certain circumstances? I know I do. Perhaps your energy soars when you experience new people, places, or concepts; or perhaps you enjoy the comfort of those things tried and familiar. In any case, all of your experiences will be heightened by a strong, vibrant mind and body. Fitness is the key to living your life with vitality.

Baby boomers are the first truly health-conscious generation. We were young at the beginning of the fitness revolution and have enjoyed a front-row seat to its numerous incarnations. We bought Jane Fonda's first workout videos and joined health clubs by the millions. We "aerobicized," stepped, ran, and power walked.

And we boomers aren't aging the way our mothers and grandmothers did. We have activities we want to do, goals we want to reach, and many years ahead of us to accomplish them.

As you age, you probably realize that you need to adjust your workouts to fit the demands of your maturing body, but you have no need or desire to stop exercising or switch to a program that doesn't present a challenge. You need a workout that keeps you strong, energized, and excited—one that allows you to live with vitality.

Using the Body Electric program as intended, every three days, strengthens muscles and, as a result of the muscles pulling on the bones, also strengthens bones, a strong concern of the boomer generation. Age doesn't matter. Fitness level doesn't matter. Amount of body fat doesn't matter. It's a proven fact that muscles will respond to the exercise challenge.

The Body Electric promise is this: if you challenge each muscle group and get to that precious place where you think you can't do another repetition, and you *do* one more repetition, that's worth everything. We love the challenge!

The Body Electric Fitness Formula

The beauty of the Body Electric program is that it can be accomplished at home with a few sets of dumbbells, an exercise mat, a kitchen timer, and your commitment. You are encouraged to continually "up" the challenge by increasing the amount of resistance (weights) used, with the priority being correct form.

The Body Electric fitness formula is straightforward and really quite simple: perform each of twelve exercises for three and a half minutes every three days. For example, if you work the biceps on Monday, you will schedule another biceps workout by Thursday. Taking more than three days between workouts for a particular muscle group may cause you to take a backslide that will impede your progress. The goal is to "hit the wall," or fatigue the muscles, in a relatively short period of time. The last few repetitions should be totally challenging.

After just a few workouts with the Body Electric program, you'll go from "I can't" to "I can, I *can!*"

I Like My Exercise Good 'n' Strong: The Benefits of Strength Training

The Body Electric excercises enable you to sculpt your body and create balance and symmetry. Don't be concerned about overdeveloping a particular muscle group or gaining masculine bulk instead of feminine definition. You won't! Bodybuilding extremists, both male and female, push the limits of muscle development with intense workouts using extremely heavy weights (and, far too often, steroids). You won't be turning bodybuilding into a full-time job, as they do, nor will you lift huge weights. Besides, even if you wanted to, most women are not equipped with an adequate amount of testosterone, the male hormone, to develop massive muscles.

Developing an intimate understanding of your body's strengths and weaknesses will provide a definite fitness advantage. When you fine-tune each exercise, you'll avoid injury and optimize the joys and benefits inherent in each workout session. When you're in tune with your body, you can continually monitor and refine your development by customizing the amount of weight used for particular muscle groups.

For example, your body type is categorized according to where most of your fat is stored. Therefore, if you are pear shaped, with wide hips and narrow shoulders, the Body Electric program provides the tools to shape and define your shoulders, giving your body a more balanced silhouette. If you are apple shaped, with large breasts, narrow hips, a thicker middle, and a flat rear end, the Body Electric program has exercises for you as well. I will show you how to effectively strengthen your abdominal and gluteus muscles to make you flatter in the front and more shapely in the rear. We will have no flat, droopy rear ends—not on my watch!

The basic shape of your muscles is genetic. Your biceps may form a peak, as mine do, when flexed; or they may have a more rounded appearance. As you increase your strength and muscle tone, you will definitely see a change in the shape and tone of your muscles. Regardless of your genetic makeup, what you *will* see is a stronger, revitalized, and shapelier you.

Consider the perennial garden as a metaphor for maintaining your own physical landscape—your body—and it becomes apparent that whether you grow apples or pears, a healthy level of fitness

Exercise your *will*power: I *will* be healthy! I *will* be fit! I *will* be strong!

can be maintained throughout your lifetime with vibrancy, energy, strength, and beauty—if you *tend* it.

Approach This Program with Resistance: A Set of Three-, Five-, and Eight-Pound Weights

I view all movement as reflected on a continuum of aesthetics and athletics, with varying degrees of power, grace, and discipline. Movement can be as artistic as ballet, as profound as yoga, or as essential to our health and well-being as aerobic and resistance-type exercise.

Exercising with resistance (weights) just a few hours a week is an investment with predictable returns, regardless of your age or fitness level. The benefits of regular participation in the Body Electric program include improved muscle tone, bone density, joint mobility, balance, metabolism, and youthful vitality. Exercise—aerobic, stretching, and muscle toning—performed on a regular basis can halt and sometimes even reverse the physical degradation associated with aging. You'll add years to your life and life to your years (cliché but true!).

With Body Electric there are no complicated schedules or charts. Exercise variations are offered to work all twelve major muscle groups, followed by exercise-specific stretches. The Body Electric exercises include variations to accommodate every fitness level from beginner to advanced, with photos and written instructions clearly defining the movements.

If you have an injury in one area, go lighter for the muscles involved, but please don't penalize your entire body for that one frailty. My exercise variations include positions standing, sitting, and lying on the floor, so you can work around any limitation. You can readily customize the Body Electric program, ensuring an enjoyable and successful exercise experience.

Truths and Consequences

With weight training, you can gain muscle and lose fat as you age rather than the other way around! Exercises with weights can also help stimulate bone formation and delay the progress of osteoporosis, and they are also beneficial for people suffering from a wide range of medical conditions, including heart problems and arthritis.

You will maintain a vibrant level of fitness by acknowledging the following truths and their consequences:

- **Truth.** The bone and muscle you build through exercise requires ongoing maintenance.
- **Consequence.** It is easier to maintain muscle and motivation than to regain it. You can overcome a week with no exercise, but a prolonged period can equate to months and even years of aging.

- **Truth.** Always strive for correct form; endurance will follow naturally.
- **Consequence.** Minor form infractions that remain unchecked over time can result in injury to the muscles and joints.

- **Truth.** The tug of muscle against bone, which occurs during toning exercises, sculpts the muscles and helps promote bone formation. In combination with a healthy, calcium-rich diet, the bone loss of osteoporosis *can* be slowed down.
- **Consequence.** Osteoporosis, the condition of brittle bones, is responsible for more than 1.5 million fractures annually, including 300,000 hip fractures (as reported by the National Osteoporosis Foundation). Osteoporosis is a skeletal disease in which bones have lost minerals, particularly calcium, rendering them fragile, weak, and susceptible to fractures.

- **Truth.** Starting at about age forty, our bodies naturally lose almost half a pound of muscle each year and replace it with the same amount of fat because of a slowing metabolism. Exercising with weights doesn't just stop this process—it actually reverses it.
- **Consequence.** If you don't do something to stop this fat-for-muscle substitution process, by the time you're eighty, about a third of your muscle will have been replaced by fat. You will gradually lose your ability to perform independently the daily life activities that you now take for granted.

- **Truth.** Strength training will actually help you lose weight as more muscle equates to a livelier metabolism. Muscle is metabolically active—that is, it burns calories at a fast rate, even at rest. So your goal is to gain more muscle, not lose it, as you age. The more muscle you have, the more calories you will burn, and the less likely you are to gain body fat. Be sure to include aerobic workouts to reduce body fat overall. Learn more about the benefits of aerobic exercise in Chapter 8.
- **Consequence.** Drop twenty pounds by severely restricting calories alone, and you will lose ten pounds of muscle. Moderately restrict calories and do regular strength training, and you'll lose fat and gain shapely muscle. Be sure to adjust your food intake so you lose weight gradually, at a rate of no more than two pounds per week.

Knowing Right from Wrong

You may choose to eat fatty foods, drink alcohol in excess, smoke cigarettes, live a sedentary existence, and basically ignore all of the health information and warnings that come your way.

However, you know that is wrong, and renewed motivation is probably the reason you're reading this book. That's right!

Give yourself plenty of credit for "right" behavior—food and activity choices that support your health and well-being. You may be one of those people who benefit from reinforcing positive behavior with rewards. You may choose to celebrate a job well done with a shopping spree; however, a success that critically affects the quality and length of your life is truly its own reward.

> "There is nothing whatsoever that does not become easier when one is accustomed to it."
>
> —SHANTIVEDA, EIGHTH-CENTURY INDIAN MONK

Change for Good

We are all creatures of habit. Have you experienced being in an exercise class where the participants claim ownership of "their" piece of real estate? Some set claim to the front row, others to the back row, and some closer to the door. And if someone else unknowingly takes their spot, beware! I have seen it all. A young woman who regularly participated in my class offered to sell her first-row spot. (I *think* she was kidding.)

Stay motivated and don't get into an exercise rut. Vary the equipment and routines used to work each muscle. Even the smallest change in a movement or movement sequence will create a dynamic difference. On the other hand, repeatedly performing the same movement incorrectly can result in injury. Do it correctly, and the outcome will always be positive.

Simply put, healthy people make healthy choices. Each day we are granted opportunities to change, for good. New beginnings are exciting, hopeful, and unlimited.

Linda's Story

I recently received an e-mail from Linda, a longtime viewer of my show. Linda's e-mail began, "Lo and behold, I found you again on television, after all these years, and I was compelled to contact you. You still look terrific, and you still inspire." I liked that part. Linda continued, "I was one of your first converts, way back when, and you actually changed my life." Linda shared that she had been going through a tough time while raising young children. "When I first experienced the Body Electric program, I had never before worked out, but you inspired me, and somehow I knew that fitness was something that was controllable."

I was struck by Linda's reference to fitness being controllable. Linda's ongoing relationship with fitness had become a dependable constant in her life that supported her health, both physically and mentally. "This became a part of my life and made me feel empowered. A lot has happened since those days, but I have always held on to that basic principle." Linda ended her message with, "A day doesn't go by that someone doesn't comment on her disbelief that I am pushing sixty! Just had to take a moment to thank you."

The Process to Strengthen Muscles and Bones

It is *never* too late to start exercising, because as you age, your muscles—including your heart—do not lose their ability to be conditioned. The human body will always respond to exercise, regardless of age or physical condition. The key to a successful exercise program is to make the most of your body and develop the strength to take life on with vitality.

Muscle Growth

Exercises using resistance, like those you'll find in this book, gently overload the muscles. Your body's normal reaction to a challenging exertion results in increased muscle stamina and strength. In addition, the pull of the muscles on the bones creates stronger bones with increased density.

Your muscles recover and build during periods of rest, with muscle soreness generally at its most intense within the first two days following your workout. This delayed reaction is referred to as delayed onset muscle soreness, or DOMS. Don't be concerned about this—it means your workout is working. If the soreness interferes with daily life, though, you probably overdid it and need to use lighter weights and pay more careful attention to form.

It is a good idea to alternate the muscle groups worked to ensure adequate time to allow for the tissue to repair. As a general rule, it is most productive to work a muscle every three days.

> You are only as old as you let yourself be.

For a Sore Muscle, Rest Is Best. Yes, you may exercise a muscle on successive days, provided that there is no soreness. However, a lack of soreness may indicate that you are not adequately challenging your muscles. This can be the result of using weights that are too light and/or exercising with incorrect form. Expect a learning curve—it's part of the process.

Respect an Injury. There will be occasions when it is in your best interest *not* to exercise. Always respect an injury. Taking quick action—whether it is a soft tissue injury, such as a sprain or strain, or a bone injury—can reduce pain, swelling, and possibly longer-term complications. The key steps are known as RICE, an acronym for:

- **Rest.** Rest the injured area for forty-eight hours.
- **Ice.** Apply a cold pack (a bag of frozen vegetables also works well) to the injured area for twenty minutes at a time, four to eight times per day. Avoid having the ice in direct contact with your skin.
- **Compression.** Bandage an injured ankle, knee, or wrist to reduce swelling.
- **Elevation.** Elevate the injured area above the level of your heart.

Note that severe injuries, such as obvious fractures and dislocated joints, or prolonged swelling and/or severe pain require immediate professional medical care.

Exercise should be joyful and its own reward. However, if you are clearly ill and your body is saying *no* to exercise, listen to your natural instincts. To address a suspected bout of laziness or the blues, I suggest that you invoke the five-minute rule: exercising for five minutes may be all that you need to become motivated. An additional bonus is the mood-elevating benefit that follows. Your pituitary gland releases substantial quantities of endorphins, which are chemicals that can block sensations of pain and produce overall feelings of well-being—just what the doctor ordered!

Form over Function

Designers and architects subscribe to the theory that form follows function, linking the form of an object with its intended purpose. In the realm of fitness, I subscribe to the idea of form over function, because if the form's not right, the function won't function.

Attention to correct form during exercise intensifies the good results and at the same time protects you from injury. Yes, your goal is to overload and fatigue your muscles. And, yes, your form must be meticulously correct before proceeding to a more intense level. You risk injury to your muscles *and* joints by compromising correct form to gain increased intensity. Here is another analogy: consider making good time but heading in the wrong direction. In other words, advancing too quickly with poor form does not benefit you physically or mentally—and may actually be detrimental.

I won't ask you to refer to complicated charts or count repetitions, sets, breaths . . . anything! Personally, I find counting very tedious and boring, and I don't want you to be distracted from your job of paramount importance: executing the movements with precise form.

During the workout, I will ask you to continuously take physical inventory, evaluating your body from head to toe. Furthermore, picturing the muscle's action in your mind's eye creates mental imagery that serves to intensify your exercise experience. To be totally involved in your workout, both physically and mentally, is a definite fitness perk as you are transported to the here and now. And, whenever possible, exercise in front of a full-length mirror. It is the next best thing to working with a trainer. Another plus: you may like what you see.

You will learn to identify anchor points for each exercise to maximize the safety and efficacy of the movement. Anchor points ground you and contribute to your stability. For instance, pressing down, or anchoring, your shoulders while working them enables you to fatigue your muscles without sacrificing the integrity of your form. Each time you exercise, use the opportunity to improve, even perfect, your technique.

You will probably tighten your grip on the dumbbells as the muscles of your upper body become fatigued. Gripping the weights too tightly causes the blood to pool in your extremities—

your fingers. Be sure to relax your fingers as much as possible to allow the normal flow of blood.

For a Safe, Effective Workout . . .

I can't stress enough—OK, I'm nagging—the importance of performing every movement with correct form before increasing the resistance. With that said, it is also critical to your continuing development to periodically increase the amount of weight used and to incorporate different exercise variations to keep your mind and muscles stimulated. When restarting exercise following a break or leave of absence, discipline yourself to begin with lighter weights, working with them until you are certain that you can move forward with meticulous form.

No discussion about correct form would be complete without my telling the story of the robins that nested on top of the lantern on my porch. Mother robin sat on her beautiful blue eggs until four babies hatched. Each day, the chicks gained girth, feathers, and confidence. I soon noticed that only two chicks remained, and they were poised to leave the nest. Suddenly, I witnessed a flurry of feathers as the little robins spread their wings and took off in glorious, graceful flight. I could hardly contain my excitement as I shouted loud and clear, "Good job, robins! Nice form!"

You, too, shall soar!

Structuring the Program: All Exercise Sequences Are Not Created Equal

The exercises in this program are presented in a dynamic combination, with each exercise designed to add intensity to the next. For instance, experience has taught me that working the pectoral muscles before other upper-body exercises serves to add intensity to the exercises for the biceps, triceps, deltoids, and back muscles. A dynamic exercise sequence often results in quantum increases in intensity and effectiveness.

I promise that you will create toned muscles, without bulk, by adhering to the Body Electric formula: light resistance with multiple repetitions. (To create larger, thicker muscles, body-builders use heavy weights in sets with fewer repetitions.) As your muscles adapt and strengthen, you will want to increase the amount of resistance used to accomplish the desired level of muscle fatigue, a sure sign of s-u-c-c-e-s-s!

It is easier to maintain muscle than to regain it. However, "muscle memory" makes it easier to regain it than it was to create it. A week's vacation is acceptable, but a prolonged break from exercise can lead to bone and muscle loss equivalent to several years of aging. "Use it or lose it" is a true phenomenon.

When circumstances cause an interruption in your workout schedule, you will most likely experience a temporary loss of muscle. However, the operative word is *temporary*, as you can always make up losses by working forward toward your desired fitness level. That is reassuring.

How Often Should I Exercise?

You may find that it is more convenient and realistic to have a twenty- or thirty-minute workout each day, varying the muscle groups exercised so that all muscles are addressed on a regular schedule. Or perhaps you would prefer a one-hour full-body routine every third day. You may maintain the status quo by exercising less frequently; however, exercising on a regular schedule encourages steady gains in muscle tone and strength.

It is imperative that you schedule daily exercise sessions to accomplish the toning, aerobic, and stretching exercises that will move you toward your fitness goals. I teach three one-hour muscle-toning classes each week at the YMCA in Orchard Park (a suburb of Buffalo). In addition, my goal is to perform forty-five to sixty minutes of aerobic exercise four to six days per week (*phew!*).

The day often gets away from me—I'm sure you can relate—and I find myself rushing to leave my office to get to the gym on time. The truth is that if I didn't have to be at the gym on time to teach my class, I probably would not make it there as often.

Please think of me the next time you consider missing your scheduled workout. You must establish discipline to accomplish your fitness goals. Schedule your workouts realistically, and then insist that you and other family members honor this time. A disciplined lifestyle recognizes that actions have consequences. Often, it is the difficult choices that propel you toward positive goals.

When Should I Exercise?

People are always asking me when the best time to exercise is, and my answer is always the same: the best time is whenever you have the time. That said, there are some advantages to working out at different times of the day. If you work out in the morning, your metabolism gets a boost that lasts throughout the day, and you have more control over your time. If you work out in the afternoon or evening, your muscles and joints are warmed up and more flexible, and the exercise may be more relaxing. If not performed too close to your bedtime, it will help you to wind down. Another option is to split your workout into several sessions during the day.

Equipment: What You Need for the Workout

The beauty of the Body Electric program is that the exercises can be effectively accomplished at home with a minimum amount of equipment, all of it inexpensive. The rest of this chapter discusses what you will need.

Comfortable Workout Clothing

Workout clothing is most comfortable when it moves with you without constraint. You might choose clothing with a relaxed fit or, conversely, a form-fitting outfit that stretches when you move, such as fabric containing Lycra (spandex). Clothing that binds at the waist, hips, knees, or anywhere else will limit your range of motion. Also, I encourage you to wear garments that inspire grace—performing the workout in your underwear or sleepwear may not be the best choice!

Athletic Footwear

The Podiatry Network (podiatrynetwork.com) suggests the following guidelines when selecting an athletic shoe:

- Choose a comfortable athletic shoe, such as a cross-training shoe, that provides arch support and makes you feel that you're standing on a solid foundation.
- All shoes are constructed over a form called a *last*. The shape of the last can follow more or less of a straight line. Choose a last that follows the shape of your foot.
- Consider athletic shoes that are relatively rigid in the heel portion as heel stability is of prime importance.

- Twist the shoe with both hands to be sure that it is fairly flexible, or "twisty," in the forefoot area. If the forefront portion of the shoe remains too rigid, your big toe will be unable to flex as the heel comes off the ground during walking and running. Adequate movement of the big toe joint is important for normal foot function.
- Your feet and the shoes you wear can have a major effect on your body mechanics. Place the shoe on a firm, flat surface and check to be sure that the back of the heel is relatively perpendicular to the surface. An angle in one direction or another could indicate a defect in the shoe.
- Put your hand inside the shoe and check for prominent seams or other irregularities that have the potential to cause irritation.

Wearing the same shoes every day will magnify a small problem. Rotating a couple pairs of shoes at a time can be helpful in prolonging the comfort of your feet and the life of your shoes.

Some years ago a gentleman friend remarked that by just looking at my feet, he would not know in what direction I was headed. Of course, this was somewhat of an exaggeration, but in truth, years of studying ballet and dancing on point had rendered my toes a pathetic jumble of hammertoes and burgeoning bunions. To make matters worse, I began ballet training at an early age, while my toes were still developing. My ongoing joke with a dear friend was that she would swap her beautiful feet for my toned thighs. I said no deal and continued my futile search for the perfect pair of "glass slippers."

But, alas, I was no Cinderella. So, after careful consideration, I opted for corrective surgery on all ten toes. A well-qualified podiatrist performed the surgery, and it was a very positive experience. I had very little downtime. I continued teaching muscle-toning classes, making accommodations for my recovering toes.

I was even inspired to produce a video, *Getting Better,* for people who can't *stand* to exercise. All of the exercises presented in the sixty-minute program are performed in positions seated in a chair or on the floor.

Please note that you should explore nonsurgical options before considering corrective foot surgery, and your own physician will help you make that decision. In many cases, a properly designed intervention, such as an orthotic device, can eliminate pain and improve mobility without surgery. I continue to regularly use orthotics in my shoes to improve my body mechanics. You may need a prescription for custom-made orthotics, or you may find that a less-expensive store-bought model works just fine.

Towel or Exercise Mat

A well-cushioned exercise mat is preferable so that you don't feel the floor during floor exercises. It is never a good idea to exercise on a hard surface without cushioning. You will create an unnecessary obstacle that prevents you from doing your best.

Kitchen Timer

This basic kitchen gadget is used to time each exercise segment, allowing you to fully concentrate on maintaining correct form while increasing the intensity. I will ask you to set the timer for three and a half minutes per exercise. This number is not random or arbitrary. My finding, based on nearly thirty years of teaching experience, is that a given movement, performed with correct form and adequate resistance (workload), will effectively fatigue the muscles during this time period.

When performing an exercise that requires you to work each arm or leg individually, time each limb separately. (If you choose to play the television or radio during your exercise session, promise me that you will keep your focus on maintaining correct form.)

Honor your time to exercise as sacred, and ignore everything in your environment that rings, whistles, or buzzes—except for your kitchen timer. Just know that when the buzzer goes off *this* time, it's not about your pot roast.

Dumbbells

Your strength and vitality will fluctuate from day to day. Therefore, having dumbbells available in varied weight increments allows you to customize each workout. Body Electric features exercises using relatively light weights with multiple repetitions to create muscle tone rather than bulk. Begin with sets of three-, five-, and eight-pound weights. If you have never exercised with resistance, you may want to begin without dumbbells, so that you may focus on practicing correct form. Keep your equipment in a conveniently accessible spot, perhaps an attractive basket in your living room, so that it is always calling your name.

Begin each exercise with weights that provide a challenge while allowing you to maintain correct form. You can always switch to a lighter set if the fatigue compromises correct form. As you become stronger, you have the option to increase the resistance by combining weights. You can crisscross the dumbbells in your hand, but resist the urge to weave your fingers through the weights.

You can purchase dumbbells at sporting goods stores or at most discount-type stores. They generally retail for $1.00 or less per pound. I advise against improvising with water bottles, food cans, and the like, as they are not ergonomically suited to the movements, and they will cause you to compromise your form and perhaps stress your joints.

Leg Weights

Leg weights are an option to add intensity to lower-body exercises. I recommend that you purchase leg weights with a strap long enough for placement above the knee as well as at the ankle. Choose leg weights that are variable, which means that you can add resistance as your endurance increases . . . and it will!

Small Rubber Ball

A small rubber ball is a useful tool to promote proper body alignment and add intensity to particular exercises. Please note that I am not referring to a weighted ball (medicine ball) but rather a playground-type ball (seven to nine inches in diameter) that is available at most local sundry or discount stores.

Water, Water, Water!

Remember the days when people (yes, men *and* women) exercised in plastic suits to sweat away the pounds? Unfortunately, the weight loss was due to decreased fluid rather than decreased body fat. Exercising in a hot, humid environment will make you naturally sweat more with greater losses of water and electrolytes. It is important to replace fluids as they are lost to prevent dehydration.

Water makes up about 60 percent of your body's weight and is critical to carrying out the normal functions of every system in your body. Dehydration, or lack of water, indicates an insufficient amount of fluid in the body to transport nutrition and oxygen to the tissues.

It is clearly important to drink the right amount of the right fluids for peak performance and safety during exercise—before and after also count. The American College of Sports Medicine suggests that it is preferable to drink plain water or fluids without sugar, caffeine, or alcohol. And drinking fluids cooler than air temperature encourages faster absorption.

If you are not drinking pure water, you need to read labels. So-called energy drinks are high in sugar and caffeine with the addition of exotic herbal ingredients such as guarana, taurine, ginseng, and ginkgo biloba—say *what?* Sports drinks fill a different niche in that they are formulated to replenish electrolytes and other nutrients lost during exercise lasting longer than ninety minutes. Have plenty of fluids on hand before, during, and after each workout. Once you feel thirsty, you are already dehydrated, so the trick is to stay hydrated from within and drink fluids *before* you are thirsty. Eight cups of fluid daily is a general guideline.

Let's raise a glass to your health!

CHAPTER 3

Maintaining Muscle Mass and Strength

I n the 1950s it was fashionable to present a body that was tight, smooth, and lifted. But back then, rather than investing the time and energy to develop natural muscle tone, most women depended on girdles to smooth their lumps and flatten their bumps. My beloved Aunt Ethel would not have dreamed of leaving her house without the proper foundations. You can be sure that the best part of her day was returning home and getting out of those hot, restrictive, uncomfortable undergarments. What a grind!

Fitness legend Jack LaLanne took a radical approach when he suggested to his 1950s television audience that daily calisthenics rather than girdles would keep housewives trim. Women had "come a long way, baby," from the original corset with bones, lacing, and hooks that was favored in the 1800s. Most women were still a long way from making exercise a part of their daily life, but they were finally becoming aware that it took more than just the latest fad diet to maximize their body's potential.

Zero to Proactive

You *have* to be proactive to maintain your vitality. To do nothing is to invite the aging process. I, for one, recognize that aging is a reality, but I'm surely not going to put out the welcome mat.

Most people don't think they look their age because the signs of age such as gray hair, weakened vision, and wrinkles are revealed subtly, over time. Have you ever noticed that the people who tend to ask, "Would you believe I'm fifty?" are the ones that often look ten years older? I am a proud sixty, with a sound mind and body—verification from others is flattering but unnecessary. Your age does not define you as a human being, but the age-related loss of muscle, known as sarcopenia, will.

Like arthritis and osteoporosis, sarcopenia is a serious degenerative condition and has the most dire effect on folks who lead a sedentary lifestyle. Your strength is directly proportional to the amount of muscle in your body. Strong muscles contribute to joint stability, the prevention of common postural problems, and agility for quick maneuverability. Therefore, basic movements such as your ability to rise from a chair, even walk across a room, and perform daily routines are profoundly affected by muscle loss.

Increased Muscle = Increased Metabolism = Reduced Body Fat

Muscle drives your metabolism—it is your body's most metabolically active tissue. You can't lose with increased muscle and metabolism, unless you are referring to the loss of body fat. Do the math:

- One pound of fat burns about three calories per day.
- One pound of muscle burns thirty or more calories per day.

A calorie is a unit of measurement that tells you how much energy a particular food provides to your body. Excess calories not needed as fuel are stored as fat. Continuing the same level of activity—or nonactivity—will increase your ratio of

More muscle burns more calories.

body fat to muscle. You can reverse this process with proper exercise and sound eating habits.

Your body stores blood sugar, or glucose, in your bloodstream and also in your liver and muscles. Consume less sugar, and you will naturally reduce the glucose levels in your bloodstream, liver, and muscles. Your body will burn glucose, or blood sugar, its preferred energy source, before it starts to burn body fat. Exercise, along with proper nutrition, results in your body using fat as fuel more quickly during your workout.

Muscle Works

Your muscles are always in a state of flux—growing and shrinking. For instance, dieters who don't get enough nutrition, namely protein, will experience muscle breakdown, particularly between meals. The faster the weight loss, the greater the loss of protein. Your body will adapt to the lower calorie intake and respond with a slower metabolism. Eventually, you will stop losing weight and your body composition will shift to a ratio of less muscle and more fat. You *can* break this unhealthy cycle. Weight training can restore muscle tissue that has been lost over the years; proper nutrition, especially the right amount of proteins (such as chicken, beef, fish, and eggs; and plant protein sources including various nuts and seeds, grains, vegetables, and legumes—particularly soybeans) and complex carbohydrates (such as vegetables, oatmeal, potatoes, rice, and pasta), will help to build and protect your muscles. The quickest way to lose weight, and keep it off, is to build muscle, which, in turn, speeds up your metabolism.

Exercising with weights works to build muscle by forcing your body to heal the damage to muscle cells that your efforts create. Your muscles rebuild with protein to make the cells stronger.

> The most powerful therapy for counteracting the effects of aging on the muscles is exercise.

Exercising the large muscle groups, such as the gluteus, legs (hamstrings and quadriceps), chest (pectorals), and back, with progressively greater resistance has the most potential for restoring lean body weight and raising the metabolism, even hours after exercise. (Aerobic exercise burns fat during exercise; on the other hand, anaerobic exercise, such as strength training, utilizes fat for hours *after* exercise.)

Do More to Do More to Do More, Ad Infinitum

You have to exercise to create an upward spiral of health, strength, and vigor. Your most powerful exercise strategy for optimal health must include a combination of weight training and aerobic exercise. While aerobic exercise serves to strengthen your heart and lungs, activities such as brisk walking, running, and swimming are not sufficient by themselves to prevent sarcopenia. Only exercises with progressively challenging resistance will increase muscle mass.

Many of the symptoms of aging can be prevented or reversed by counteracting decreasing levels of natural human growth hormone (HGH), which plays an important role in the regulation of muscle mass, bone density, and metabolism. In addition to diet and sleep patterns, resistance training is probably the largest contributor to growth hormone release. Muscle overload

Arlene's Story

"I have been following Margaret's Body Electric program for over four years. I had been suffering for years with chronic back pain. As the pain increased, I became less and less active. I suffered from fatigue as well. I had given up on all exercise including walking, which I had always loved. Both my doctor and my daughter, a competitive bodybuilder, kept encouraging me to begin a workout routine focusing on muscle strengthening. I heard about Margaret's classes at a gym close by. I had never been in a gym before but finally pushed myself to try her class, starting with very low expectations. Margaret easily recognized my weakened condition and patiently eased me into the program. I was not able to use any weights for the first several sessions and took baby steps from there.

"I fell in love with the program but more importantly with the way that Margaret passionately teaches it and encourages all who participate. I soon became very committed to getting stronger and feeling better. I slowly progressed with heavier weights and soon started a walking program again! I lost twenty-five pounds, most of which I have been able to keep off, and I became stronger than I have been in many, many years.

"I often wonder what I would be like today if I had not met Margaret. Although I still deal with chronic pain, it is not nearly as debilitating. My one huge regret is that I did not know of Margaret and Body Electric much earlier in my life."

causes the release of lactic acid that, in turn, triggers the secretion of HGH—an unmatched antiaging force.

Even if you have led a basically sedentary life, you can end up with more muscle mass and strength than you had in your thirties and forties by following the Body Electric program. Maintaining your body's muscle throughout your life is equivalent to winning the lottery *plus* discovering the pot of gold at the end of the rainbow *and* never having a bad hair day.

The Journey to Fitness

Understandably, we are most comfortable with things we find familiar. For example, I never learned to ride a bicycle as a child, and my experience of learning to ride as an adult has been somewhat awkward and intimidating. I have become more comfortable on the bike, but you will still *never* see me riding a bike near anything that moves. And that is a loss for me.

Keeping in mind my experience—or lack of experience—of riding a bicycle helps me to relate to people who have limited exposure to exercise. You have to accept that new skills feel awkward until they are practiced repeatedly. Do you remember how different your first day of school felt compared to subsequent weeks, when the routine had become more familiar? I think you understand my point.

The Aesthlete

Don't try to find the word *aesthlete* in any dictionary—or even try to pronounce it. It is a word that I coined to define a combination of *aesthetic* and *athletic*. I have long held a fascination with the dynamic relationship between music, graceful movement, and exercise. My training in ballet has had a major influence on my "muscle with grace" style. When I lead a class, I often observe participants who are totally invested in the experience with closed eyes and perfect form. Fitness just doesn't get any better than that.

Perhaps you, too, have studied ballet or have had the pleasure of attending a ballet performance. Certainly you have been moved by the effortless grace that propels each dancer. What you don't see are the intense isometric or static muscle contractions that help the dancer maintain proper alignment—the strength behind the grace. In an isometric contraction, tension is developed in the muscle, but the muscle does not shorten and there is no joint movement. In my experience, static muscle contractions feel like a simultaneous push and pull of a particular muscle group. Try this:

1. Press your shoulders down.
2. Be sure that your shoulders are square (symmetrical).
3. Anchor your shoulders in place while you reach forward with your arms and hands as if you are trying to touch an object that is just beyond your reach. Remember to reach with your arms and not your shoulders.

Dust off your tutu. Maybe we'll have that recital after all.

Your Fountain of Youth

Spanish explorer Ponce de León set out in 1513 on a voyage to discover the fabled Fountain of Youth. Unfortunately, he never found it, though he did discover Florida in the process. If only Ponce de León knew then what we know now—that discovering the Fountain of Youth is as easy as exercising with weights. And you, too, may discover a new state—of physical harmony and vital well-being.

CHAPTER 4

Flexibility and Stretching

Maybe, just maybe, if we stretched more, we would be less uptight, and peace would reign throughout the land. That may be wishful thinking, but at the very least we would be able to tie our sneakers when we're ninety! Flexibility, or the lack thereof, is probably the single most important factor affecting our quality of life as we age. The pain and stiffness of aging begin as temporary tensions that become learned habits. But don't assume that with aging you will automatically lose your flexibility. You *can* counterbalance the effects of aging so that your physiology is quite a bit younger than your chronology. When you stay flexible, you'll be able to live with vibrancy, energy, and independence.

The Benefits of Stretching

Over the years, we develop habitual ways of using our muscles to move and position ourselves. Poor posture and a lack of flexibility may be the result of a legitimate medical problem or may be the result of limited stretching and improper body alignment. When muscles get tight and stay tight, they cease to be elastic and they restrict movement. That sense of restriction, or stiffness, often leads to disuse. Disuse causes weakness and tightness, which in turn causes a vicious cycle of more disuse, weakness, and tightness.

Your muscles may also become tight and short due to overuse (resulting in

Touching your toes should not require a stretch of the imagination.

injuries such as tennis elbow or tendonitis) or underuse. If nothing is done to lengthen stiff and short muscles, they continue to tighten, restricting circulation and impeding the removal of toxins. And a short and tight muscle is more prone to injury. Ouch!

It is easy to take your physical capabilities for granted, until there is a problem. Your long-term goal should be to maintain your range of motion so that you can continue to accomplish everyday tasks, pain-free. This goal is totally realistic if you are willing to commit to a regular schedule of careful stretching. The benefits of a stretching program will be readily apparent, and you will experience increased comfort as your body moves with fluidity and balance.

Stretching is the best way to maintain muscle and joint flexibility. When you stretch regularly, you will also reduce general muscle tension. A prime benefit of stretching is that it increases the distance your limbs can travel before injury occurs to the muscles and tendons.

Runners, in particular, suffer from painful hamstring injuries. These sprains and strains—even tears—of the muscle fibers are most likely the result of tight, inflexible hamstring muscles creating an imbalance with the opposing quadriceps. Every muscle in your body has an opposing muscle. It stands to reason that your muscles will experience less fatigue when a contracting muscle does not have to exert as much force against a flexible opposing muscle.

Here are some tips for stretching efficiently:

- **The best time to stretch is following your workout, when your muscles are warm.** Stretching, as part of an effective cooldown, helps to alleviate the soreness of post-workout muscles caused by microscopic muscle tears and accumulated waste products (lactic acid). Stretching lengthens the individual muscle fibers, thereby increasing blood circulation, which helps to remove the waste products, and reducing muscle soreness. A warm bath or shower will also suffice to warm you up, if you prefer.

- **Stretch your muscles back to their resting length after each exercise.** Exercising your muscles with resistance, as we do in this program, results in stronger—and temporarily shorter—muscles. Shortened muscle fibers are more easily injured. Be sure to perform the muscle-specific stretches I offer following each exercise.
- **Stretch every third day for five to ten minutes to keep your muscles supple.** If your muscles are particularly tight, you may want to perform gentle stretching more often.
- **Static stretching gradually lengthens a resting muscle.** As the word *static* implies, there is no bouncing or reaching once you have stretched your muscle to an elongated position. Hold the stretch for fifteen to thirty seconds. As always, focus on correct body alignment.

Look forward to the cooldown as a reward for a job well done. Stretching should be peaceful, both physically and mentally. Quiet your mind, breathe deeply, and r-e-l-a-x.

Mind Bending: Mental Flexibility

Experience has certainly taught me that life is always in a state of flux—that circumstances and situations change all the time. What I know for sure is that an open and flexible point of view creates a youthful spirit. I first learned to "roll with the waves" when

I attended Lamaze classes in preparation for the birth of my son, Todd. The instructor used the ocean's waves as a metaphor for labor contractions: you can face a large wave head-on and it will surely knock you down, or you can ride with the wave for a more positive outcome. This lesson has served me well over time.

> "A mind that is stretched by a new experience can never go back to its old dimensions."
>
> —OLIVER WENDELL HOLMES

A respected teacher once told me that I could accomplish anything, within reason, if I truly dedicated myself to its pursuit. I considered myself to be mathematically challenged, so I returned to college, twenty-five years after I graduated, to prove that teacher right and to finally put to rest my fear of numbers. After spending a good deal of time in the math lab, where tutors were readily available, I earned an A and a B, respectively, in my first two algebra classes. By the third course, which had a relatively advanced curriculum, my brain was on algebra overload, and as my professor graciously remarked, I *earned* my D. I actually celebrated that D as proof positive that I could persevere in subject matter that I had formerly perceived as impossible to comprehend. Start an exercise program—or a new career. You are never too old to create or adapt to change in your life. Do you define yourself in terms of boundaries such as like and dislike, can and can't, or right and wrong? Maybe it is time to rethink the rules. That idea was put forth in a popular catchphrase first used in a 1971 ad for Alka-Seltzer, "Try it, you'll like it," as it was later in Nike's "Just do it!" In either case, the message is to put aside your preconceived notions and try something new—you just may like it!

Your Body Has Hundreds of Joints Designed to *Move*

Your muscles, joints, ligaments, and tendons perform in harmony so that you can walk, jump, bend, and, if you're lucky, even dance the tango, all effortlessly.

Your tendons are tough bands that connect your muscles to your bones and help your muscles exert a pulling force; ligaments connect your bones to each other and provide additional support. The shape of your tendons is inherited—what you get is what you get. You will have a greater potential for muscle mass if your genetic package features shorter tendons and longer muscles. On the other hand, you will be more naturally proficient in actions such as running and jumping if your gene pool includes the longer-tendon/shorter-muscle package. Case in point: competitive runners have "great genetics" if their Achilles tendons are particularly long in relation to shorter calf muscles. For the rest of us, stretching increases the length of muscles and tendons, resulting in reduced muscle tension and increased range of movement.

Over time your tendons and ligaments will retain less water and become stiffer and less able to tolerate stress. As these changes occur, you may notice more restricted and less flexible joint motion. You have to stretch, actively, gently, and regularly, to maintain your flexibility at *any* age. That is why gentle stretching is an integral part of the Body Electric program.

My maternal great-grandparents immigrated in 1915 to America from Eastern Europe with twelve children (two more were born in the United States after they arrived!). My grandmother, one of the older siblings, suffered a vitamin D deficiency in her formative years, which resulted in the bone disease known as rickets. Rickets caused a softening and weakening of her bones, which bowed her legs and eventually caused painful arthritis in her knees. My grandmother's weight gain due to inactivity certainly didn't help matters. (We now know that even modest weight loss can have a significant impact on reducing knee-joint stress.)

My grandmother always bemoaned her fate, thinking how different her life would have been with "good" legs. I vividly remember her spending her later years sitting in a chair on her patio. Today things would have been different for her. Rather than being told to stay off her feet, she would have been encouraged to get—and keep—moving, well into her old age. Research has shown us, time and again, that an active life is one of the easiest and most important ways to keep our bodies acting and feeling young.

When Arthritis Is an Issue

Shock-absorbing cartilage on the ends of your bones allows for ease of movement, *except* when the cartilage is affected by disease (rheumatoid arthritis) or by wear and tear (osteoarthritis). Range-of-motion exercises, which gently stretch the joints as far as possible in all directions to preserve mobility, are advantageous for everyone but *essential* for anyone who suffers from arthritis. (Please refer to the cooldown exercises in Chapter 18.) In addition, strengthening the surrounding muscles provides increased joint support and stability. An additional perk: joint movement transports nutrients and waste products to and from the cartilage, the material that protects the ends of the bones.

In the case of osteoarthritis, the cushioning cartilage begins to break down from a lifetime of use, and the resulting discomfort is a *real* pain and may be inconvenient—but it is definitely not a showstopper.

Susan's Story

"Fitness has always been an important part of my life. However, my activity choices were limited to low-impact exercises, due to a childhood spine deformity. More recently, my physician shocked me with the diagnosis of Lyme disease following a sudden onset of severe joint pain, muscle weakness, and the resulting depression.

"After almost two years of misery, I was introduced to Margaret Richard's Body Electric fitness program. Margaret's methods of exercising with resistance and exercise-specific stretches were the perfect catalyst I needed. By participating three to four times per week, I gradually grew stronger, and my pain was reduced, which improved my mental and physical state in every way. The Body Electric program has been nothing short of lifesaving for me!"

Some women experience aching joints, muscles, and tendons during perimenopause and menopause. This pain, not associated with trauma or exercise, may be due to the effects of fluctuating hormones on the immune system. Being informed helps you to be an advocate for your own health and welfare. Consult a medical professional to rule out osteoporosis, arthritis, and fibromyalgia. Knowing the questions to ask your health provider is key to receiving the best treatment.

Bend the Rules for Flex Ability

Medical experts agree that moving your joints with exercise can actually relieve aching and soreness. Exercising with weights strengthens your muscles, and stronger muscles help support and protect joints affected by illness or injury. Relieving joint stress increases flexibility and endurance and reduces stiffness. And that's just for starters.

YOU HAVE OPTIONS

- If you have arthritis, applying heat packs to your joints or taking a warm bath will stimulate joint lubrication.
- If holding dumbbells causes discomfort in your fingers, hands, or wrists, Hand Irons by Ironwear may be just what you need. They are adjustable "gloves" that are weighted with rubber and require no holding. For more information, see the Ironwear website, ironwearfitness.com.
- If you are just beginning, it might be helpful to focus on performing the exercises with correct form and without weights.
- If you have limitations, check out the different exercise options I offer. Many of the movements can be done seated or lying down rather than standing. It is most important that you get moving. Start slowly and do what you can. In time, you will be able to do more.

CHAPTER 5

Healthy Bones for a Healthy Life

I challenge you to find a woman over the age of forty who isn't concerned about osteoporosis. With all the books and articles about how to prevent it, and the advertisements touting the latest drugs to treat it, osteoporosis is definitely front and center when it comes to women's health.

Osteoporosis causes a loss of bone minerals, density, and strength and is characterized by porous, fragile bones. Women are four times more likely to develop osteoporosis than men, who also experience "change-of-life" symptoms, although relatively mild ones. With so many of us living twenty to forty years beyond menopause, osteoporosis—literally, porous bone—is a real health concern that threatens millions of people.

Your bones are living tissue, and they're hard at work 24-7, supporting your muscles and organs. Like Bob Vila, they are constantly in the process of "remodeling"—getting rid of the old stuff and building new. When you're younger, up to about age thirty, the building of new bone outstrips the losses. The result is a net gain. After about age thirty, you will most likely strike a pretty good balance, losing about as much bone as you are gaining, maintaining the status quo. By the time menopause rolls around, diminishing estrogen levels accelerate bone loss; you may lose bone tissue at a rate that can rapidly equate to a serious net loss—not good for the portfolio!

Scientific research has proven that even women with severe osteoporosis can be helped, at any age. And preventing bone disease is certainly much easier than correcting bone loss after it occurs. Of all the proven positive lifestyle habits, only one will help you transition through menopause by strengthening your muscles and bones and improving your body's calcium metabolism. What is this magic formula? *Weight-bearing exercise.*

Weight-bearing exercise causes your bones and muscles to work against gravity while they bear your weight. When you lift weights, the tension caused by the pull of your muscles on your bones stimulates the production of new bone tissue—you can turn that net loss back into a balanced equation, even a net gain.

What You Can Do: Screening and Prevention

Osteoporosis is a silent disease that is difficult to diagnose. Hopefully your bones are solid and strong and will remain that way. A diseased bone viewed through a microscope presents a very different picture, with tiny holes and spaces. You might not even know you have osteoporosis until a minor injury causes you to suffer a fracture, especially in your hip, spine, or wrist. That's why you should be aware of the early warning signs of osteoporosis, which include periodontal disease, increased curvature of the spinal column, loss of height, or pain in the middle or lower back. Compression fractures of the spine, a specific kind of bone break involving the vertebrae, can cause symptoms that range from nonexistent to severe. The classic image of an aged woman with a dowager's hump, the not-so-attractive upper-back deformity, is an image of a woman whose body has suffered the ravages of vertebral fractures and bone loss.

Your health-care provider can use an x-ray that measures bone mineral density to determine if you are at risk for osteoporosis. The National Osteoporosis Foundation recommends that women over age sixty-five be screened annually. The most accurate test, DEXA, is an x-ray that measures bone density in your spine and hip. The test itself is quick and painless, and most insurance plans will cover it. It is important to check your height on a yearly basis, too, as losing stature can also be indicative of osteoporosis. See "Risk Factors for Osteoporosis" on the following page to determine if you're at risk.

Risk Factors for Osteoporosis

According to the National Osteoporosis Foundation, you are at increased risk for osteoporosis if any of the following are true:

- You are female.
- You are older than fifty.
- You have a family history of the disease.
- You have a personal history of fractures as an adult.
- You are Caucasian or Asian.
- You are small-boned and weigh less than 127 pounds.
- You smoke cigarettes.
- You drink too much alcohol.
- You consume too little calcium.
- You get little or no weight-bearing exercise.

Certain risk factors, such as age, gender, and genetics, are not subject to change. They are what they are. Others, such as tobacco and alcohol use, diet, and exercise, are known as modifiable risk factors, things you have the power to change. You must know by now that I'm all about empowerment: to create the best self you can be, at midlife and beyond. And if you are still smoking, stop already!

Stay Upright with Strength, Balance, and Flexibility

It is never fun to take a fall, but if you have osteoporosis, avoiding falls is paramount. Even a seemingly minor fall can lead to a fractured wrist, hip, or spine. Hip fractures almost always require hospitalization and major surgery and can result in prolonged or permanent disability. Exercising with weights definitely increases your ability to circumvent a disabling fall.

Strength

Regular weight-bearing exercises that force you to work against gravity have clearly been shown to minimize bone loss, especially after menopause. Maintaining muscle strength so that you can move your body about with ease and grace is one aspect of fall prevention; having strength to rise from a chair, climb stairs, and lift objects can mean the difference between standing tall or doing not much at all. Exercise has profound effects on the strength and integrity of your bones. You *have* to add a weight-bearing component to your fitness regime to maintain and even rebuild bone. Aerobic exercises such as swimming and biking don't provide enough stress on the long bones of the body to stimulate bone growth; walking, climbing stairs, and dancing *are* weight bearing and good for your bones. (See Part 2 for strengthening exercises.)

Balance

One side of your body, usually the less dominant side, may become more easily fatigued when you are exercising. Working to correct this disparity leads to a greater ability to respond to shifts in body weight caused by unexpected obstacles—like a dog underfoot—and a stronger, more stable stance. Balance can be improved with practice, so do test yours frequently. Try to balance on one foot, or practice heel-to-toe walking: for each new step, place the lead foot directly in front of the other.

Flexibility

Increasing your range of motion enables you to move your body more effortlessly and in the ways that you want—for example, bending down to speak to a child or stretching up to reach a shelf—and plays a significant role in your body's ability to respond to everyday tasks and challenges. For a variety of exercises that promote flexibility, refer to Chapter 18.

All Together Now—Nutritional Synergy

Getting calcium from food improves your bone density more than taking it as a supplement, probably because of other micronutrients in the food and a little thing called synergy. *Synergy* means that the parts of things, taken together, are really equal to more than the whole. In other words, you can't just pull out one ingredient and get the same benefit. Consider Sonny without Cher, the Beatles without John, or calcium without vitamin D—it's just not the same! A well-balanced diet rich in calcium and vitamin D contributes to the health of your bones and works synergistically to make your skeleton stand strong and tall.

> "Care for yourself at all times, rather than only after you become ill."
>
> —DEEPAK CHOPRA

Calcium

The human body requires more calcium than any other mineral. The adult human body contains about 1,000 to 1,200 mg (milligrams) of calcium, with at least 99 percent of the calcium found in the bones and teeth, giving them strength and rigidity. Getting enough calcium from food or supplements is essential because the human body doesn't produce it.

The National Osteoporosis Foundation's Recommendations for Daily Calcium Intake

Age 19 to age 49 . . . . 1,000 mg

Age 50 and over. . . . . 1,200 mg

Postmenopause . . . . 1,200–1,500 mg

Let's revisit your bone "portfolio"—every day that your body doesn't absorb enough calcium to meet its needs, your body "borrows" calcium from your bones to support the proper functioning of your heart, muscles, and nerves and for blood to clot. If this net loss continues day after day, your bone density will steadily decline over time, increasing your risk of osteoporosis.

The amount of calcium that your body can absorb from your digestive tract into your body's circulation depends on several factors including:

- **Your vitamin D intake.** Adequate vitamin D intake from food and sunlight must be present for calcium absorption.
- **Your age.** It is very important to maintain strong and dense bones to minimize the effects of calcium loss after age forty.
- **The bioavailability of the foods you consume.** Bioavailability determines how much of the calcium you consume is actually absorbed and utilized by your body. In the United States, milk, yogurt, and cheese are the major contributors of calcium in the typical diet. (Nonfat and low-fat dairy products have the same amount of calcium as the full-fat variety.)

Some vegetables naturally contain phytic acid or oxalic acid, which are substances that can interfere with optimal calcium absorption. While these substances do not affect the absorption of other calcium-containing foods eaten at the same time, you may have to eat several servings of foods, such as spinach, sweet potatoes, and beans (soybeans are better absorbed), to obtain the same amount of calcium as is present in one cup of milk.

Following are some good food sources of absorbable calcium:

Plain low-fat yogurt (1 cup) . . . . .448 mg
Sardines, canned in oil (3 ounces) . . . . .324 mg
Milk, skim (1 cup) . . . . .316 mg
Cheese, mozzarella, part skim (1.5 ounces) . . . . .310 mg
Orange juice, calcium fortified (1 cup) . . . . .300 mg
Soy milk, calcium fortified (1 cup) . . . . .300 mg

○ **The total amount of calcium that you consume at one time and whether the calcium is taken with food or on an empty stomach.** Before adding a calcium supplement to your diet, consider your total daily intake of calcium from all foods, including those fortified with calcium. The UL (tolerable upper limit) for calcium is 2,500 mg per day.

Calcium Supplements. It may be necessary to take supplements to ensure that you meet your daily calcium requirement. Calcium exists in nature only in combination with other substances. These substances are called compounds, or calcium salts. The two best calcium supplements are calcium carbonate (such as Tums and Os-Cal) and calcium citrate (such as Citracal). Both types are readily available, contain large amounts of elemental calcium, and dissolve well in the body. Remember that absorption from supplements is best when the supplement is taken in doses of 500 mg or less throughout the day, with meals. I discovered this last bit of advice the hard way. Like many post-menopausal women, I'd been taking calcium and doing weight-bearing exercise to stave off osteoporosis. After having several normal bone density tests, over several years, I was surprised to have a test that reported osteopenia, which while not a disease does indicate low bone density and can lead to osteoporosis. After consulting with my doctor, I learned that I was mistakenly taking my daily 1,500 mg dose of calcium all at once, instead of spreading it out over the day in doses of no more than 500 mg. What a difference that made! The next year I was back in the normal range for bone mineral density.

Vitamin D

Vitamin D is manufactured in your skin through exposure to ultraviolet rays from sunlight and is necessary for the absorption of up to 65 percent of calcium. Like calcium, vitamin D levels decline with age, with bone loss generally greater in the winter. The National Osteoporosis Foundation recommends that women age fifty or under get 400 to 800 IU of vitamin D per day and that women fifty or older get 800 to 1,000 IU. Good sources of vitamin D are fortified milk, egg yolks, saltwater fish, liver, and supplements.

Lose the Fat, Keep the Bone

Because of the obesity epidemic, health-care professionals often encourage their patients to reduce their body fat to lower blood cholesterol, blood pressure, and other risk factors for cardiovascular disease. However, the potentially negative effect of weight loss on your bones should also be an important consideration. It is well known that rapid weight loss—particularly in women over fifty years of age—can take a toll on bone density.

In general, people with low body weight face a greater risk for reduced bone mass and bone fractures. Younger women can also develop osteoporosis, usually due to a poor diet, low body weight and the resulting estrogen loss, calcium deficiency, and malnutrition. Studies show that overly restrictive dieting at any age affects the bones sooner than later, increasing the risk for osteoporosis and fractures throughout life.

If your doctor recommends weight loss, discuss your concerns about bone loss and request an evaluation of your bone density.

The best way to lose weight with bone health in mind is to do the following:

- Lose weight very gradually—a maximum of one to two pounds per week.
- Maintain healthy nutrition—include foods with calcium and vitamin D.
- Focus on increased activity rather than food deprivation.
- If you need to reduce calories, decrease the fat calories and keep the protein.

Don't kill yourself to be the thinnest babe on the block. A diet that contains vital and wholesome foods will support a stronger life force. Be physically active, eat a nutritious diet, and live a healthy lifestyle. You'll do very well!

CHAPTER 6

Boning Up on Body Mechanics

Why Posture Matters

Observe the ballet dancer whose balance appears effortless. In reality, it is only through intense and exhaustive training that the dancer is able to create balance by keeping her body in perfect alignment.

Correct body mechanics and posture allow you to function safely and efficiently, with minimal strain on your muscles, joints, and ligaments. And, if like most of us your body mechanics are less than perfect, developing adequate muscle tone makes you less vulnerable to injury.

The strength of your body's core—the back, stomach, and other torso muscles—is essential to healthy posture, because it acts as a central stabilizer for the rest of your body. When the muscles of your pelvis, lower back, and hips are strong, they work in harmony and provide the support needed to protect against lower-back pain, muscle injuries, and poor posture. Fortunately, the human body is very adaptable, and over time, you can unlearn bad habits—and replace them with good habits.

Poor Posture Can Be a Pain in the Neck

Good posture involves training your body to stand, walk, sit, and lie in positions where the least strain is placed on supporting muscles and ligaments during the normal course of movement. This is a simple but very important way to keep the many crucial structures in your back and spine healthy.

Your backbone, or spine, runs from the base of your skull to your tailbone and is composed of thirty-three vertically stacked bones (vertebrae) that are cushioned by disks. Add spinal fluid, and you would think you have ample protection for your spinal cord and nerves. However, it is the way you carry yourself—

your posture—that most significantly protects your spine from injury.

Your spinal column is designed to curve naturally, both forward and backward. Your spine has two natural curves, which work like shock absorbers to help your body maintain balance and to move your spinal column through its full range of motion. Your lower back (lumbar curve) bears most of your weight, so proper alignment of this section can prevent injury to your vertebrae, disks, and other portions of your spine.

CHECKLIST FOR IMPROVED POSTURE

- **Suck and tuck.** Producing the "Body Electric" television show requires that I constantly multitask, simultaneously focusing on the viewers, my fellow dancers, the exercises, the music, the cameras, and so on. The one thing I never forget to do is suck and tuck, which is my way of checking my posture. I visualize a neutral—fairly straight but not rigid—line from my head to my tailbone and perform a head-to-toe posture "inventory" to be sure that my body is in proper alignment: chin up, neck long, shoulders down, chest lifted, abs and gluteus tight, knees relaxed. (I also wear the hat of editor, so if, heaven forbid, my suck-and-tuck grows lax, I have the option of switching to an alternate camera shot— thank goodness—but I try not to let that happen!)

> "A good stance and posture reflect a proper state of mind."
>
> —MORIHEI UESHIBA

- **Head straight up, chin in, ears over shoulders.** If your head and neck project forward, your back automatically goes out of alignment. Your goal is to position your head over your neck so that you can look directly ahead without feeling tension in your neck.

Another great side benefit of keeping your head up and your ears, shoulders, and hips aligned is that you appear more confident, which provides a boost to your ego. I used to be extremely shy (cross my heart) and often looked down to avoid making eye contact with others. I can remember times when I would duck into the restroom to catch my breath if I sensed a guy was looking my way. After many years of looking down, I had to retrain myself to stand tall and bring my ears in line with my shoulders.

○ **Shoulders down.** A dear friend of mine, a psychiatric nurse, cared for a patient who continuously pressed his shoulders down with his hands—so that he wouldn't float away. While this man was clearly suffering from something other than gravity depravity, the image left me with a lasting impression: pressing your shoulders down provides a stabilizing anchor for your entire body.

Tension in the muscles that lift your shoulders and support your back is the primary cause of most shoulder pain. I've noticed that the shoulders lift at the first sign of fatigue during exercise. To relax your neck and shoulders anytime, do the following:

1. Stretch your head and ear toward your shoulder to alleviate stiffness in your neck.
2. Rotate or shrug your shoulders to ease tightness.

Minor adjustments in the alignment of your neck, shoulders, and back make a dynamic difference in the health of your back as well as your appearance. You can also minimize a less-than-flattering silhouette by increasing muscle tone. With appropriate posture (when standing), it should be possible to draw a straight line from your earlobe, through your shoulder, hip, and knee, and into the middle of your ankle. Did you ever try to walk like a model by balancing a book on your head? Today's supermodels who strut the catwalk with shoulders thrown back and hips forward—often done while teetering on super high heels—would be hard-pressed to accomplish the book-balancing feat.

- **Chest lifted, or DYOBL (do your own breast lift).** Standing without slouching, rounding your shoulders, or exaggerating the natural curves of the spine instantly gives you a more youthful and energetic appearance. Furthermore, you can DYOBL (do your own breast lift) by lifting your chest while standing tall. The late humor columnist Erma Bombeck advised that the most flattering position for females when sleeping and lying down is with one or both arms overhead. She also suggested that if you want to have an honest look at your naked self, stand before the mirror wearing only boots.

   By the way, the best way to sleep is on your side with your knees bent, a pillow to support your neck, and a firm mattress.

- **Abdomen and gluteus muscles contracted.** When you're standing straight, make sure your abs and glutes are gently contracted. My ballet studies taught me that standing straight does not mean holding your spine rigid like a toy soldier. There is always a slight curvature to the spine, maintaining the pelvis in a neutral position, not tilted forward or backward. "Neutral spine" is the natural position of the spine when all body parts are in correct alignment.

   The most common muscle imbalance leading to back pain is due to weak abdominal muscles and an excess of belly fat that causes the abdomen to protrude. Severe back pain is the direct result, as the abdomen is straining rather than supporting the back. Exercise can help reduce and even eliminate muscle imbalances. You can exercise weaker muscles to catch them up to stronger ones and work to correct and maintain overall stability. After the initial correction of bad posture habits, these movements tend to become automatic and require very little effort to maintain.

- **Knees relaxed.** Alleviate tension in your back by relaxing your knees. Unlocking your knees lets you more easily accommodate the natural S curves in your back. Next time you are standing in line at the grocery store and you feel tightness in your lower back, try flexing (bending) your knees while simultaneously tightening the muscles of your abdomen and gluteus to bring your pelvis into a more neutral position. (Be careful not to exaggerate this position by tilting your hips.)

- **Feet slightly apart.** Good foot posture helps to put your entire body into balance. Place your feet slightly apart, with one foot positioned slightly in front of the other and knees bent just a little bit (not locked). Lift the arches of your feet slightly, so that your body weight is supported by the outside edges of your soles. And when you stand or walk, your toes should point almost straight ahead.

For a long time I searched for the perfect shoe, until I had my epiphany—I did not have the perfect feet. According to the American Orthopedic Foot and Ankle Society, "We're all susceptible to foot and ankle injuries, but we can reduce our risk by wearing properly fitting shoes that conform to the natural shape of our feet." It is truly basic, common sense.

Orthotics, custom-made inserts for your shoes, can be worn with well-fitting footwear to address certain issues of your feet and lower body. Custom orthotics are prescribed by a physician and are usually one aspect of a therapy program. By the way, pedicures don't qualify as a therapy, but they sure do look good.

Heidi's Story

"As a trained dancer, I became familiar with the Body Electric program on television as a way to stay in shape when I was unable to dance. After the birth of my first daughter, fourteen years ago, I herniated a disk in my lower spine and feared that I would always have limited movement. Fortunately, my back stabilized and I was advised to resume exercise without limitations. I truly believe that the overall strength I gained through the Body Electric program helped me to overcome my back injury. When I first attended Margaret's classes, I could barely make it through a given exercise. However, my strength and endurance increased quickly—and it was obvious. My delicate 'ballet arms' became more muscular and toned. I love building muscle with weights. I guess you could say I'm addicted. The mind-body connection is incredible. I learned that the limits we have are generally self-imposed. Margaret reminds us that we can actually enjoy the temporary discomforts that come with progress by reframing the experience as beneficial, manageable, and ultimately, desirable."

If you are a "Body Electric" television viewer, you know Heidi as the wonderfully toned and fit woman who often joins me for the workout. She is also a very good sport about laughing at my silly jokes.

A Stiff Price to Pay

Have you ever noticed that as people age they lose the normal curve in their spine and walk stiffly? Without curves, your rear end appears to have no dimension. That's a definite red flag, warning you to begin a strengthening program to improve your posture and reclaim your once shapely rear end.

Back support is especially important for people who spend many hours sitting in an office chair or standing throughout the day. With a sedentary job and weak back muscles you risk soreness and injury when you perform an exercise as mundane as gardening or lifting a package.

According to the National Institute for Occupational Safety and Health, "Back injuries cost American industry 10 to 14 billion dollars in workers' compensation costs and about 100 million workdays annually. A healthy lifestyle—attention to posture, conditioning and body mechanics, avoiding obesity and smoking, and minimizing emotional stress—will take you a long way toward maintaining a healthy back."

> "Physical fitness is not only one of the most important keys to a healthy body, it is the basis of dynamic and creative intellectual activity."
>
> —JOHN F. KENNEDY

Over time, the stress of poor posture can change the anatomical characteristics of the spine, leading to the possibility of constricted blood vessels and nerves, as well as problems with muscles, disks, and joints. All of these can be major contributors to back and neck pain, as well as headaches, fatigue, and possibly even concerns with major organs and breathing. Your awareness of the importance of correct posture is the first step toward correction.

Ergonomics is the process of changing your environment to support healthy body mechanics. Small modifications in your work environment can make a huge difference. It is surprising to realize that sitting puts eleven times more pressure on your vertebral disks than lying down. Because the increased pressure on disks and subsequent back pain is not immediate, we often blame too much standing for our lower-back pain when the real culprit is tired back muscles.

THE RIGHT WAY TO SIT

- Sit in chairs with straight backs or lumbar (lower-back) support.
- Maintain your ears, shoulders, and hips in a straight line, with your head up and your stomach pulled in.
- Sit back in your chair.
- When sitting at a desk, think in terms of right angles (90 degrees, or the shape of an *L*). Your knees should be at 90 degree angles when the soles of the feet are touching the floor. Your back and thighs should form 90 degree angles when your body is sitting properly in a chair, with your legs uncrossed. Your wrists should be straight, with your elbows at 90 degree angles when your hands are on the desk or keyboard.
- Turn by moving your whole body rather than by twisting at your waist.
- Try to avoid sitting in the same position for more than thirty minutes.
- Move to the front of the seat of your chair and stand up by straightening your legs. Avoid bending forward at your waist.

And, If It Happens . . .

The best position for relief when your back hurts is lying on your back on the floor with pillows under your knees and your hips and knees bent. This takes the pressure and weight off your back. Just relax.

CHAPTER 7

Belly Fat and Hot Flashes

*Why Menopause Changes
Your Body Shape*

The simple truth is that we over-forty-and-fabulous sisters have to make lifestyle changes to accommodate midlife. The decline in hormone production during menopause causes aging and can also lead to a host of degenerative problems. Whether you are experiencing perimenopause, menopause, or postmenopause (that would be me), knowledge brings understanding and understanding is empowering.

Perimenopause is a completely normal process that usually occurs between the ages of forty-five and fifty-five and lasts four to five years (it can sometimes last even longer). It is the period when you still have a period but are beginning to experience some symptoms of menopause. You are still ovulating, but your body may react to an increasing imbalance of estrogen and progesterone with symptoms that include mood swings, night sweats, insomnia, and weight gain, particularly in the midsection—your abdomen and hips. It's not exactly a party, but it doesn't have to be a train wreck either. It is a good bet that anxiety, smoking, and/or carrying too much body weight will intensify your symptoms. A healthy lifestyle will provide you with immeasurable benefits—but you already know that.

When you haven't had a period for twelve consecutive months, you've reached *menopause*. Your ovaries produce much less estrogen and progesterone and don't release eggs. This is a natural biological reaction and doesn't change your status as a strong and vital woman who will continue to be youthful, sexy, and receptive to life's spectacular gifts.

You'll spend the rest of your life in what is known as *postmenopause*. Continue to define yourself as youthful, energetic, and strong. Here's to making those years the best ones ever!

Menopausal Fat or Fiction?

If you were an interplanetary traveler, you would surely question why we earthlings purposely sabotage our good health and well-being by making unhealthful choices. We know that a high-fat diet lacking essential nutrients combined with insufficient exercise can lead to type 2 diabetes, cardiovascular disease, certain types of cancer, and a generally compromised existence. Go figure!

How knowledgeable are you about the relationship between menopause and increased body fat? Answer the following questions true or false:

1. If you are a woman with a waist circumference of thirty-five inches or greater, you are at an increased risk for obesity and its related health problems.
2. Many women gain a minimum of five pounds during the transition to menopause.
3. Lost muscle is typically replaced with an equal amount of fat.
4. Muscle-toning exercise performed on a regular basis can rebuild lost muscle and burn calories at the same time to help you lose weight.
5. The fat that once was concentrated in your hips and thighs may settle above your waist and in your abdomen during menopause.
6. Abdominal fat cells are more metabolically active—and more potentially dangerous—than the fat cells on your hips and thighs.
7. The classic apple-shaped figure is associated with excess belly fat and an increased risk for health-related problems such as elevated cholesterol, insulin resistance, and heart disease.

8. During the menopausal transition you may need to eat less and exercise more, just to maintain your current weight.

9. A muscular, athletic woman may have a high BMI (body mass index) *and* a healthy weight because muscle weighs three times as much as fat.

10. You must starve yourself to avoid gaining body fat during menopause.

Answers 1 through 9: absolutely true.

Answer 10: false, false, false!

Perhaps you, too, have gained those extra five-plus pounds of body fat while going through the hormonal roller coaster of menopause. A one-size-fits-all diet will not provide the long-term solution you are seeking. A professional dietitian will consider your unique nutritional needs before recommending a course of action to help you achieve success.

There is a direct correlation between improving your diet and improving your health. As a general guideline, I recommend that you refer to the DASH diet (Dietary Approaches to Stop Hypertension), which has been proven to lower blood pressure, reduce cholesterol, and improve insulin sensitivity. The DASH diet, which formed the basis for the new USDA MyPyramid, is "rich in fruits, vegetables, low-fat or nonfat dairy, and also includes grains, especially whole grains; lean meats, fish and poultry; nuts and beans." For more information about the DASH diet, see dashdiet.org.

My BFF (Belly Fat and Flashes)

Whether you are careening toward "the change" or have already experienced it, your ongoing goal should be to maintain youthful strength and flexibility, as well as a healthy ratio of body fat to lean muscle. Exercise cannot prevent menopausal symptoms, but it can decrease the frequency and severity of a host of symptoms that may affect you in varying degrees.

My first experience with menopause came in 1998, the year I married Jack and moved from Florida to western New York. The timing of my move north couldn't have been better. That Thanksgiving I had my first hot flash, in my mother-in-law's kitchen, with ovens full of holiday fare. I quickly discovered that winter's true beauty lay in the "meat locker" effect—cool refreshment anytime you step outside. Take heart, my menopausal sisters of the South! Your years spent tolerating a hot, humid environment have helped to prepare you for "the change."

Over the next few years I began to notice a thickening around my waist and back. It showed no mercy! At midlife I had gained more wisdom, understanding, compassion, discipline, awareness, serenity, muscle tone, bone density—and, yes, b-b-b-back fat! I wasn't eating more (maybe just a little) or exercising less (maybe just a little less aerobic exercise in the winter). At the time, I wished I could have filmed my "Body Electric" shows from the neck up. However, that would not have worked for an exercise program. I *had* to go public with my menopausal body fat—and believe me, viewers noticed.

> "Every human being is the author of his own health or disease."
>
> —BUDDHA

The "Before" Pictures

As a young woman, I never did sprout hips. For most of my life, I viewed my shape as similar to that of a teenager—slender and narrow. I always thought it would be interesting—like a science project—to see how my body would react to the changes brought on by menopause. Unfortunately, it began to feel like an experiment gone awry. Shortly after entering the menopausal zone, I gained ten pounds of body fat (none of us are immune!), which displayed itself around my abdomen and rendered my favorite clothing uncomfortably snug.

I was intent on maintaining a healthy reputation with my "Body Electric" audience and, most important, with *myself*. I had always seen my body as fit and lean and had a difficult time identifying with being thick in the middle. I viewed my weight gain and body-shape shift as a challenge—*and* an opportunity for success.

My mission was to reduce my body fat overall without losing muscle (very important!). I chose to document my progress with the mandatory "before" pictures. I arrived at the photographer's studio equipped with my wardrobe, makeup—and additional body fat. I instructed Carol, the photographer, and Cathy, the makeup artist, to create a tasteful picture with no special effects. (I did not plan to morph into an unrecognizable goddess in the "after" photos!) Our session went something like this:

CAROL: Don't mind the fat. It smoothes out the wrinkles.
CATHY: Stand sideways so you can show how the back of your skirt hikes up.
CAROL: Let's use natural light—it shows *everything*.

They agreed that a photo of me in flat shoes would be even more unflattering. My pride cast the overriding vote, and I chose the high heels. The three of us shared raucous laughter. However, I had the last laugh because although I had added some midsection body fat to an otherwise fit frame, I was secure in the knowledge that after years of participation in my Body Electric program, I had toned muscles, dense bones, and youthful vitality.

If you are wondering about my "after" pictures, just turn the pages of this book.

Body Fat: The Good, the Bad, and the Ugly

Jack Sprat could eat no fat,
His wife could eat no lean.
And so betwixt the two of them,
They licked the platter clean.

Poor skinny Jack and his overweight wife!

As a society, we have targeted body fat as public enemy No. 1. In reality, it is the quantity and distribution of body fat that determines whether it is beneficial or harmful to your health. Fat actually plays an essential role in maintaining the health of your body. "Essential" fat, approximately 4 percent of your body weight, is needed for a wide variety of functions, such as temperature regulation, reproduction, shock absorption, the regulation of nutrients, and the maintenance of healthy skin, hair, and nails. Another 15 percent of your body weight provides the fat storage used as fuel to get you from meal to meal.

As it turns out, having an "apple" shape, with narrow hips and thighs, as I do, presents a greater health risk than having a more curvy "pear" shape. It is a broad generalization, however, that an apple-shaped body has more of a tendency to develop visceral fat deep inside the abdomen. Even otherwise slender women can have a potbelly.

If you have a pear shape, you are certainly not immune to health risks. Waning stores of estrogen may produce middle-age spread. Even though your weight remains stable, you may notice

Don't Make Me Laugh— or Sneeze, Jump, Lift, Yell, or Cough

Please say it isn't so! Menopause can cause you to be wet and dry in all the wrong places. Here are the facts, ma'am: producing less estrogen can cause the lining of the bladder to weaken. As bladders get weaker and reaction times become slower, you become more aware of having less bladder control.

As with any other muscle, exercise can help weak pelvic floor muscles to be strong again. Kegel exercises strengthen the muscles that hold the bladder and many other organs in place. Kegels, or pelvic floor exercises, also serve to increase sexual gratification.

Exercising your pelvic floor muscles for just five minutes three times a day can make a big difference. Your doctor can show you how. The exercises for the gluteus muscles, shown in Chapter 16, can effectively incorporate Kegels. You can tone your gluteus *and* pelvic floor muscles at the same time.

You can also choose to go the route of either hormone replace therapy (HRT) or natural, bioidentical replacement therapy to address your hormonal imbalances and significantly relieve stress incontinence.

One last word: squeeze before you sneeze, jump, lift, yell, cough—or laugh.

the accumulation of body fat around your abdomen rather than your hips and thighs.

Two Kinds of Fat

There are two kinds of fat: subcutaneous and visceral. Subcutaneous, or "pinchable," fat is located directly beneath the skin and generally does not pose a threat to your health. Studies have shown that exercise frequency has a greater effect than diet in reducing this type of fat. Aerobic exercise burns calories, while muscle-toning exercise creates more muscle, which, in turn, boosts your metabolism to burn fat—even when you are at rest.

Excessive visceral, or belly, fat is located deep within the abdomen and can create a health hazard by surrounding the organs in your abdominal area and interfering with the function of your liver—including cholesterol and insulin production. Daily exercise and a diet low in saturated fat will help prevent the accumulation of belly fat and lower your risk for disease.

According to a study published in the *Journal of the American Medical Association* in 2003, there was a direct correlation between the amount of time women spent exercising and the amount of belly fat they lost. Additionally, University of Arkansas researchers found that study participants who performed ninety minutes of moderate exercise five days a week lost twice the amount of belly fat as those who just dieted. The results of these studies are not too surprising, when you think of everything we've been talking about, but the bottom line is simple: you *have* to exercise.

Finding Your Balance

Not too long ago, convention dictated the use of hormone replacement therapy (HRT) because it helped alleviate some of the less pleasant symptoms of menopause and was believed to promote bone health. But when a study was released in 2002 connecting HRT with increased risk of heart disease and breast cancer, everything changed. Today many women are turning to holistic, natural support for improved overall health and a smoother transition from perimenopause to postmenopause.

When your hormones are in balance (which is your body's natural state), you have more vitality and you look, feel, and

"Aging does not have to be nor should it be a difficult process."

—JOHN O. WYCOFF, D.O.

act younger. More important, your body is protected against some of the worst diseases associated with old age. In my quest to bring my own body to greater balance, I consulted with Dr. John Wycoff, who heads the Wycoff Wellness Center in East Lansing, Michigan (wycoffwellness .com). In preparation for our meeting, Dr. Wycoff prescribed various types of testing and monitoring to accurately evaluate my hormone levels. I was tested for the following:

- **Thyroid function.** Thyroid hormones govern the body's metabolism and development. Hormonal imbalances often trigger low thyroid function, or hypothyroidism, which is why it is more common in women than in men. Common symptoms of hypothyroidism include fatigue, weight gain, depression, and high cholesterol.
- **Adrenal function.** Cortisol is the naturally occurring steroid hormone that is secreted in response to stress. Chronic stress causes your body to secrete excessive amounts of cortisol, which, in turn, triggers stress eating and stimulates fat production deep in your abdomen. The adrenal glands' ability to function decreases with age and can result in "adrenal fatigue."
- **Ovary function.** Estrogen, progesterone, and testosterone are the sex hormones. They decline as a woman ages, with the progesterone declining most rapidly as its production is directly linked to ovulation.

Dr. Wycoff prescribed a combination of bioidentical hormones, vitamins, and herbs to address my hormonal imbalance, sluggish thyroid, and adrenal fatigue. Bioidentical hormones are biologically identical to hormones produced in our bodies. They are derived from a plant molecule that is found in soybeans and wild yams. According to Dr. Wycoff, "All women need to understand the foundation of healthy hormones begins with an appropriate diet. We are what we eat, drink, and think. An appropriate diet should be rich in fresh fruits, vegetables, and lean meats. Reducing the amount of sugar and high-glycemic foods such as breads, pastas, and potatoes is a major step in the right direction.

"Taking the appropriate supplements is also important in assuring long-term health and wellness as you transition though menopause. I find that most of my patients require a good quality multivitamin, often several per day. I also routinely recommend omega-3 fatty acid replacement. The omega-3 fatty acids, found in fish oils, may be the single most important supplement that will assist women as they move through perimenopause and into menopause.

"We must strive to find the optimal way to improve our health and wellness. This is not always about finding the hormone level that is 'normal,' but finding the level that is optimal. The goal of bioidentical hormone replacement therapy is for you to enjoy continued good health as you age and to feel full of wellness, health, and vibrancy for years to come."

It is in your best interest to make a personal and informed decision regarding your approach to wellness, menopause, and, ultimately, your quality of life. Your health-care provider may decide that you need hormone supplementation to support your ongoing well-being. Or you may be able to relieve your symptoms by fine-tuning your nutrition, exercise, and stress-relieving techniques. My heartfelt advice is to be knowledgeable, take a whole-body approach to your midlife health, and establish a balance—*your* perfect balance—of diet and exercise.

I continue to maintain my muscle tone with the Body Electric program, and I incorporate aerobic conditioning with early-morning forty-five- to sixty-minute walks in the park with my dog—our daily ritual. (I'm still on the treadmill in winter, sans dog.) In addition, I periodically consult a registered dietitian for updated nutritional support. It was hit-or-miss in the beginning—and then, success! We came up with a plan of nutrition custom designed to accommodate my lifestyle, food preferences, and midlife nutritional needs. I am determined *not* to blame my waning hormones for the poor food choices and activity levels that have a major effect on postmenopausal weight gain.

With a revved-up diet, daily walks, and, of course, the Body Electric muscle- and bone-strengthening program, I have sailed through menopause, needing only the occasional carefully controlled midcourse correction. It was what it was, and I am what I am—a fit, strong, and vital woman. I want the same for you.

CHAPTER 8
Aerobic Conditioning

Your heart is an incredible organ. Heart muscle—also called cardiac muscle—makes up the wall of the heart. Throughout life, it beats an average of some seventy times per minute, or four thousand times per hour, pumping about five liters of blood each minute.

The overload principle applies to the heart in the same way it applies to any other muscle in the body—you have to subject it to loads greater than those to which they are accustomed. Conditioning this hardworking and reliable muscle with aerobic exercise is a critical part of your fitness equation. Aerobic exercise is the key to cardiovascular health. The American Heart Association recommends that to attain a high level of cardiovascular fitness, you should gradually work up to exercising on most days of the week for thirty to sixty minutes at 50 to 80 percent of your maximum capacity. The popular formula for estimating your maximum heart rate is 220 minus your age. (At fifty years old, your maximum heart rate is 170. Your aerobic range would be a pulse of 85 to 136 beats per minute.)

One thing I hear over and over again is that people have trouble sticking with their exercise program, so I always emphasize that practicality must be an important consideration in your choice of aerobic activities—you will then have a higher probability of keeping at it. And what could be more practical than simply putting one foot in front of the other? Regular walking is an obvious aerobic choice—easy on your joints, easy on your pocketbook (your only expense is the cost of a pair of walking shoes), and easily accessible. Walking provides both physical and psychological benefits by:

- Helping you lose excess body fat and keep it off
- Reducing your risk of heart disease, stroke, and diabetes

- Keeping your joints and muscles mobile and supple
- Giving you a more positive outlook, reduced anxiety, and less depression

My mother, who walked for fitness in the early 1960s, was definitely ahead of her time. We lived on Harbor Island, between Miami and Miami Beach, and my mother was in the habit of walking around the island—very briskly—every day. She was considered somewhat of an oddity, but she continued for many years because it made her feel so good.

Following in her footsteps (pun intended!), I take a brisk walk each day. When I begin my daily walks, even before I leave my driveway, I feel simultaneously energized and relaxed. This healthy and natural high created by "feel-good" endorphins released by the brain is an added bonus of walking. Choose to invest your time and energy in an activity with infinite health benefits, and you will reap amazing rewards. In fact, many an inspiration for this book came to me during my walks.

The Key: How Far, Fast, and Frequently You Walk

To be effective, fitness walking has to be deliberate with regard to how far, fast, and frequently you walk. To continue to achieve benefits, you have to plan for a progressive overload. In other words, don't allow yourself to plateau at a comfortable level. Your goal is to continue to increase your pace, over time, and to improve your circulation by making your heart pump blood more efficiently throughout your body. Consistency is crucial so that your progress doesn't yo-yo. Your body will become conditioned to increased intensity over time but only through repeated efforts.

Walking farther, faster, or more frequently are variables; adding a hill or interspersing your normal pace with faster sprints can also up the challenge. But don't try to increase everything simultaneously—work on increasing how far you walk in some sessions and how fast you walk in others. While you are building speed, I suggest that you gauge your walks according to time rather than distance. If possible, begin with thirty-minute walks (fifteen minutes in each direction), the minimum goal for increasing cardiovascular health, according to the American Heart Association. As you become more conditioned, increase your pace to cover more distance in the allotted time.

A reasonable goal is to walk three miles in forty-five minutes, sometimes less and sometimes more. Adding a sixty-minute walk once or twice each week will definitely boost your body's fat-burning capability. Increasing your walking pace from three to four miles per hour can double the benefits. The surgeon general recommends that your thirty minutes of moderate-intensity aerobic activity can be accumulated, meaning you can do it in shorter bouts of ten or fifteen minutes throughout the day. And there is no law that says you have to begin each walk from your home or workplace. A brief car or bicycle ride can transport you to a variety of scenarios. One day you may enjoy a rural country setting, while another day you may prefer a walk around your neighborhood. I encourage you to get in your car and map out several three-mile routes, a mile and a half there and back.

Increased oxygen during aerobic exercise strengthens your heart and lungs. *Aerobic* literally means "in the presence of, or with, oxygen." Your body initially fuels the increased effort by burning excess carbohydrates. When your store of carbohydrates has been depleted, after about twenty minutes, your body will begin to use fat for fuel—going first to the regular reserves and then the harder-to-reach places. Therefore, a longer walk will definitely burn more fat and continue to do so for several hours postexercise!

Remember the following the next time you flirt with the idea of indulging in food that is loaded with fat or sugar:

- Carbohydrates, including sugar, that are not immediately used by your body for fuel are converted to fat deposits for long-term storage.
- Excess fat is stored in areas where fat deposits are already located, such as your abdomen, hips, and thighs.
- Your body depends on its fat stores to keep you alive when food is scarce. However, the possibility of imminent famine is remote to nonexistent, so stop flirting with danger. Puh-leese!

Walk First, Stretch Last

Begin and end your walk with five minutes of more casual strolling, gradually increasing the intensity of your movements at the beginning and decreasing them at the end. If you choose, you can perform some gentle stretching at about five minutes into your walk (see Chapter 4). Save the more vigorous, range-of-motion stretching until your walk is completed (see Chapter 18).

You may experience muscular aches and pains, particularly when you increase your goals. If you have discomfort (such as painful shin splints) while walking, it is important to rest until the injury has healed. Continuing to exercise with an injury will just prolong the pain. *Always* respect an injury. Be sure to schedule one day of rest each week to prevent physical and psychological burnout. You will return to your walks with renewed vigor and conviction.

Taking Physical Inventory

Your continuous awareness of your body's proper alignment will increase the benefits of your exercise. Maintaining correct form will require more attention initially, until it becomes a habit. I think of it as physical inventory. Starting with your head, move down your body, concentrating on and correcting each body part, one at a time.

- **Head.** Look ahead rather than down. Try to maintain a "stacked" position, with your ears in line with your shoulders, hips, and heels.
- **Chest and shoulders.** Keep your chest lifted with your shoulders relaxed and down. Correct form allows your arms to move fluidly. It is also useful to think about keeping your neck long and leading with your sternum.
- **Arms.** If you are like most, you swing your arms in the same relaxed and slightly bent manner whether you are taking a leisurely stroll or a brisk walk. Using your arms properly during fitness walking will increase your walking speed, which in turn increases your cardiovascular benefits. As you speed up, bend your arms at right angles (90 degrees). Move your arms forward and back in a straight line, and align the backswing with, but not behind, the side seam of your shirt. Alternate reaching each arm and hand forward (and not diagonally) across the front of your body.
- **Hands and fingers**. Do your rings get tight when you walk for fitness? Keep your hands and fingers unclenched and use the correct arm swing to alleviate a good deal of the swelling.
- **Back.** Maintain your back in a neutral position as you walk, maintaining your natural S curves.

- **Abdomen and gluteus.** Gently contract the muscles in your stomach and rear end to increase your core strength and create added back support.
- **Knees and legs.** Walk with a natural stride. Take more steps rather than longer ones. And don't tighten your knees or lift them too high.
- **Ankles and feet.** Relax your ankles so that your heel will strike the ground first. Roll through to push off from the ball of your foot and toes as your body moves forward. Don't raise your toes too high, as this may cause discomfort in your shins.

Even Horses Need Proper Shoeing

Wear appropriate, well-fitting walking shoes as this will encourage vibrant walking and limit fatigue. Shop for shoes late in the day, when your feet are their maximum size, and try on several pairs before making your decision. Your shoes should be replaced about every 500 miles. If you walk six days per week at 3 miles per day, you will walk 18 miles per week, or 936 miles in a year. On that schedule, you will need to replace your walking shoes twice per year. I suggest, instead, that you purchase both pairs of shoes at the same time so you can alternate them to prevent potential foot irritation.

Choose shoes that provide an adequately roomy toe box for your toes to widen as you push off. There is nothing more annoying than sore toes caused by

> "One can have no smaller or greater mastery than mastery of oneself."
>
> —LEONARDO DA VINCI

too short or too narrow shoes. Put your hand inside the shoe to check for protruding or rough inseams that may rub. I remember when I first snow-skied with rental boots. If they didn't fit perfectly, they created hot spots on the first day that were bothersome for the entire trip. I quickly learned that it made all the difference to own custom-fitted boots.

Choose breathable microfiber athletic socks that wick the moisture away to help your feet stay dry and blister-free. You can also use powder or petroleum jelly on your feet to minimize friction. In cold weather, add extra protection for your extremities.

Safety First!

Before moving to New York, I lived on a golf course in Florida and enjoyed my early morning walks before the sun and golfers were up. One evening, my soon-to-be husband, Jack, and I decided to take a late-night stroll. We were halfway around the course when two men approached us wearing ski masks and carrying automatic weapons. I couldn't believe my eyes, or my ears, as Jack announced, "I'll take the big one. You take the little one." (What???) My heart was pounding a mile a minute as the men identified themselves as members of a special police swat team practicing nighttime maneuvers. They asked us to leave the area. Talk about your brisk walking—we were out of there faster than you could yell "Fore!"

Safety Must Be a Prime Consideration

When you're exercising outside, consider the following safety precautions:

- Be aware of your surroundings, including what is behind you.
- The natural sounds of the environment can be soothing. However, if you choose to wear headphones, keep the volume low so that you can hear what is going on around you.
- Walk in populated areas and on the left side of the road, facing traffic.
- Carry a phone and identification.
- Leave your valuables at home.
- Wear bright, reflective clothing, particularly at sunset or after.
- Carry a bottle of water so you can keep hydrated, particularly in hot and humid weather.

Do You Walkie-Talkie?

When gal pals walk, they often engage in animated talk. Walking with a friend has its advantages. It is motivating to travel in twos and provides an extra layer of safety. If you are walking for cardiovascular conditioning, find a partner with a similar fitness level. If one of you is faster, that person can walk ahead and double back without missing a beat. To check whether you are working at the correct intensity, you should be slightly out of breath but still capable of carrying on a conversation (this is called perceived exertion). In any case, it is OK to "walkie-talkie" as long as the walkie, rather than the talkie, is the priority.

Saving Face

Collagen supports the healthy configuration of your skin; its production is naturally depleted during the aging process. You can develop muscles in other areas of your body to give your skin support and shape; however, I have found no scientific evidence

When You're Outside: Protect Your Skin

You can certainly tell the difference between skin that has been exposed to a lifetime of sun and skin that has been protected from the elements, such as the skin on the breasts and buttocks.

I grew up in Miami Beach during the late 1950s and '60s. The tourists would appear each winter eager to work on their tan. Returning home with a dark glow spoke volumes about luxury and leisure. Unfortunately, many visitors also suffered burned and peeling skin in the process. I learned, early on, to respect the sun's damaging rays. Predictably, the smooth, tanned skin of a twenty-year-old will prematurely sag, wrinkle, and discolor thirty years hence. Now the effects of the sun are well known—although many young women choose to ignore the warnings—but when we boomers were young, most of us didn't know that the glow of a deep tan wasn't healthy.

Physicians tell us that there is no safe tan; *any* tan means your skin has darkened due to the damaging, excessive ultraviolet rays. Caucasian people are about twenty times more likely to get skin cancer than African-American people, but no one is immune. Sunscreen helps but is not foolproof. In addition, the increasing depletion of ozone in the atmosphere is allowing in more UV rays. And the truth is that tanning booths can be more damaging to the skin than the sun because they use pure ultraviolet light.

Attend the skin, your body's largest organ, with this proactive approach:

to support exercise for the facial muscles as a remedy for aging skin (with all due respect to the practitioners that advocate it). I recently consulted plastic surgeon Dr. Michael Storch, a talented and well-respected plastic surgeon in Aventura, Florida (storchplasticsurgery.com). He confirmed the following:

"A regular program of exercise and stretching is definitely beneficial for maintaining vibrant health and a youthful appearance—except in regard to the appearance of your face and neck. My personal opinion is that most facial and neck exercises are

- **Stay properly hydrated.** Drink at least eight full glasses of water a day to flush away toxins and to keep your skin soft and healthy.
- **Protect your skin from the sun.** It is worth repeating that sun damage is one of the leading causes of prematurely saggy skin and facial wrinkles. Routinely apply a sunscreen with an SPF rating of 30 (why use less?) on every exposed area of your body: arms, hands, face, neck, and chest.
- **Don't smoke.** Avoid smoking at all costs. If you are currently a smoker, do whatever you can to quit. Smoking actively increases the signs of aging and is counterproductive to all healthy pursuits.
- **Use a face and body skin cream with AHA.** Over time, the epidermis (the outermost layer of skin) creates new cells more slowly, and damage to the skin by the sun thins the skin. Alpha hydroxy acids (AHAs), found in many over-the-counter skin creams, work by increasing the turnover of skin cells. Use creams with AHAs on the entire body for skin that has an all-over healthy glow.
- **Protect your skin from unnecessary trauma.** Following the onset of menopause, estrogen-deprived skin thins, loses collagen, and slows down its cell renewal. Wearing long-sleeved, sun-protective clothing during outdoor activities (such as gardening) protects against sunburn as well as unsightly cuts and bruises. (Sun Precautions' clothing offers a 30+ SPF that blocks 97 percent of UVA and UVB rays; Rit Sun Guard is a laundry treatment providing UV protectant.)

more harmful than beneficial. Equate the skin of your face and neck to that of a delicate fabric that loses its smooth and supple appearance after being exposed to excessive pulling, stretching, and general overuse.

"We are all affected by the aging process in varying degrees. The loss of skin tone as we age is influenced by genetics, diet, and the management of environmental factors such as exposure to the sun and smoking. It is up to you to decide how much of your personal resources of time, effort, money, and relaxation you are willing to devote to modifying and slowing these processes that occur over time."

Using a Heart Rate Monitor

When you're doing aerobic exercise, it's important, for maximum benefit, to keep your heart rate within a specified range. Your target heart rate zone is calculated by subtracting your age from 220 and multiplying by 50 to 80 percent. So, for example, if you're fifty years old, your target heart rate would be 102 to 136 beats per minute. A heart rate monitor allows you to measure your heart rate in real time. The monitor usually includes a chest strap transmitter and a wrist receiver that resembles a wristwatch. Some aerobic machines, such as treadmills, feature a built-in monitor that measures your heart's BPM (beats per minute) with a device that you squeeze manually. The heart rate monitor keeps you in touch with your target heart rate zone during aerobic activity and is a practical alternative to taking your pulse.

It's All About Options

It makes sense that the more vigorous aerobic activities, such as brisk walking, running, swimming, bicycling, roller-skating, and jumping rope, do the best job of strengthening your heart and lungs and of reducing body fat. However, thirty minutes of low- to moderate-intensity activities, such as pleasure walking, gardening, housework, and dancing, are also beneficial. Your primary consideration is to ensure that your heart and lungs are worked hard enough and long enough to gain the benefits of aerobic exercise but not so long that you run the risk of injury.

If you live in a more vigorous climate, as I do (how's that for political correctness!), there comes a time when you have to move indoors. The snow is poetically beautiful but is better suited for skiing than walking. On the other hand, an air-conditioned environment can be a welcomed alternative to warm and humid conditions. It is not essential to join a gym to get an aerobic workout. There are plenty of other options:

- **At-home activities** include exercise videos or DVDs, stationary biking or treadmill activities, rebounding (bouncing on a minitrampoline), stepping, dancing, or anything else that gets your heart beating vigorously for an extended period of time.
- **Outdoor activities** include walking, jogging, running, biking, hiking, and downhill and cross-country skiing. Obviously, weather-appropriate clothing is a major consideration.
- **Water activities** are dependent on whether you have access to a pool. Swimming is a very effective cardiovascular activity. It is low-impact and is often recommended for people who have problems involving their muscles or joints. Swimming has the advantage of being a full-body workout that can be of benefit long after other forms of exercise may cease to be an option.
- **Gym or health-club activities** include elliptical and cross-country trainers, the treadmill, StairMaster, and rowing and ski machines. Additionally, group fitness classes offer a variety of aerobic choices, such as dance-exercise, step, and spinning. Alternating several training methods, called cross training, will serve to increase the challenge, improve your overall performance, and provide physical and mental stimulation.

And When You're Not Exercising: The Importance of a Good Night's Sleep

For most people, eight hours of rest provides the optimal energy needed to charge their memory. Menopausal symptoms such as night sweats may interfere with your ability to get a good night's sleep, but try to get as close as you can to eight hours a night. A good night's sleep is both healing and restorative. Here's how to get yours:

- Establish a natural rhythm by going to sleep each night and waking up each day at about the same time.
- Avoid activities that are stimulating or upsetting right before bed. Watch or read the news earlier in the evening.
- Limit alcohol, caffeine, and tobacco for several hours before bedtime.

- Use your bedroom *only* for sleeping and sex.
- Create a soothing environment with pleasant colors, a comfortable mattress, and smooth sheets.
- Perform thirty minutes of exercise daily.

And if you can't sleep:

- Get out of bed to do something relaxing in another room.
- Drink warm milk or eat a slice of toast with peanut butter or a bowl of cereal.
- Take a thirty-minute midafternoon "power nap" the next day. (In Latin countries they call it a siesta.)

- **Group activities** like tennis and golf require the expenditure of large amounts of energy, while providing motivation and much enjoyment—virtues not to be underrated. However, group sports can often be less effective for aerobic conditioning as there are periods of downtime where the heart rate is allowed to slow down.

The bottom line is to get moving! Any exercise is better than none at all, and correct form is the key to realizing your ultimate potential.

PART 2

The Dynamic Exercises

CHAPTER 9

The Warm-Up

I t's all right to go from zero to sixty in under four seconds if you're driving a Lamborghini. Otherwise, putting the pedal to the metal will probably smoke the tires and cause them to skid in place.

Likewise, don't expect your body to go from zero to sixty when you work out. Even elite athletes have to do a thorough warm-up for optimal performance and injury prevention. Warming up prior to exercise provides you with that much-needed transition from sedentary to active. It prepares your body *and* mind for the more strenuous activity to follow, and it minimizes the likelihood of injury—a most important twofer.

The warm-up is so named because the movements slowly increase your body's core and muscle temperature, which effectively increases the elasticity of your muscles, ligaments, tendons, and cartilage. Your built-in temperature regulator, perspiration (OK, sweat), helps to prevent your body from overheating.

A warmed muscle both contracts more intensely and relaxes more easily. Here's how it works:

- Your muscles contract and relax as you continue to work them through their full range of motion.
- As your muscles warm up, you continue to increase the number of muscle fibers that can contract together, which places less stress on the individual fibers.
- A stronger and healthier muscle is less vulnerable to injury.

The warm-up also allows time for your heart to adjust to the increased workload. Your blood vessels dilate to assist additional blood flow to the muscles, carrying increased oxygen and nutrients, such as blood sugar and adrenaline. The endurance and performance of your muscles is further fueled by increases in your blood temperature. The warm-up exercises improve performance, but, more important, they help to prevent or reduce muscle soreness and the chance of injury.

As you age, warming up becomes even more of a necessity because your tissues become less supple and your joints retain less fluid. By activating the fluids in your joints, you reduce wear and tear caused by friction and increase your range of motion.

It takes about four to five minutes to warm up your body, depending on how tight your muscles and joints feel on a particular day. It also may take longer to loosen up on cooler days. Bear in mind that experimentation and experience with the workout will result in increased body awareness. Vary the warm-up from time to time to find what works best for you. For instance, background music may be energizing on some days, while on others, Zen-like silence may be more conducive to increased concentration and body awareness.

Always begin your warm-up gradually and be aware that your cold muscles are less elastic. More focused stretching is best done after your exercise session, when your muscles are warm and pliable with the increased blood flow. In the warm-up that follows, you will begin with gentle stretching of your head and neck and progress down your body, energizing each major muscle group. Then, with your chassis purring, you'll be revved up and ready to roll—so to speak.

Gear

- When possible, exercise in front of a full-length mirror so you can check your form.

FYI: Grace and Flow

Exercising with resistance improves your strength and balance, which facilitates your ability to move with grace.

Beginning Stance

1. Stand with your head held up straight, your chin in, and your earlobes in line with the middle of your shoulders.

2. Lengthen your neck.

3. Press your shoulders down and lift your chest.

4. Tighten your abdomen and rear end while maintaining your back's normal S curves (neutral position).

5. Relax your knees.

6. Position your feet about shoulder width apart.

Overhead Reach

1. Inhale through your nose as you reach overhead with both arms.

2. Exhale through your mouth as you lower your arms to your sides.

Head Tilt

1. Slowly tilt your right ear toward your right shoulder.
2. Anchor the movement (press down) with your left shoulder.
3. Repeat to the left.

Head Rotation

1. Turn your head to look over your left shoulder.
2. Repeat to the right.

Shoulder Shrug

1. Lift your shoulders toward your ears.

2. Press your shoulders back down to their normal position.

3. Repeat twice.

Upper-Back Stretch

1. Bring your arms forward in a circular position.

2. Separate your shoulder blades to open your back.

VARIATION

Crossed-Arm Stretch

1. Cross your arms in front of your chest, right arm over left.

2. Lift both arms as high as possible without lifting your shoulders (the movement is subtle).

3. Repeat with your left arm over your right.

Overhead Reach and Press

1. Reach your arms overhead, with hands pressed together and facing forward.

2. Gently push both arms back until they are in line with your ears.

Triceps Stretch

1. Anchor your left elbow behind your head with your right hand.

2. Push back against your arms with your head.

3. Repeat with your right elbow anchored with your left hand.

Chest Stretch

1. Clasp both hands behind your back.

2. Squeeze your shoulder blades toward each other as you reach back.

3. Lift your chest.

Side (Obliques) Stretch

1. Position your feet about shoulder width apart.

2. Bend your right knee and place your right hand just above it.

3. Extend your left hand overhead, with your left arm positioned next to your left ear.

4. Repeat on the right.

Flat Back Position

1. Place your feet about shoulder width apart and bend your knees.

2. Bend forward maintaining a fairly straight line with your head, neck, and back.

3. Press your abdomen against your back.

4. Squeeze your shoulder blades toward each other.

5. Lift your hips and tailbone. (You will feel a mild stretch in your hamstrings.)

Rounded Back Position

1. Place your feet about shoulder width apart and bend your knees.

2. Tuck your chin in toward your chest.

3. Separate your shoulder blades to open your back.

4. Round your back up and tuck your tailbone down.

5. Press your abdomen against your back.

Front Lunge

1. Assume the flat back position with both hands just above your knees.

2. Bend your right knee and center your upper body between both legs.

3. Square your shoulders so that both are facing the floor evenly.

4. Push your bent knee back to line up over your ankle (as much as possible).

5. Repeat to the left.

Side Lunge

1. Position one leg in front of the other leg with both hands resting just above the front knee.

2. Bend your front knee and keep it in line with your ankle.

3. Create a straight line (as much as possible) from your head to the heel of your back leg.

4. Press the heel of your back foot to the floor.

5. Square your shoulders and hips so that they are facing the same direction.

6. Repeat but with the back leg now positioned in front.

WHAT'S WRONG?

WRONG: The front knee is positioned farther forward than the ankle.
RIGHT: The front knee is in line with the front ankle.

WRONG: The back heel is lifted.
RIGHT: The back heel is pressed to the floor.

WRONG: The right shoulder is positioned farther forward than the left.
RIGHT: The shoulders are positioned squarely over the hips.

Calf Stretch

1. Assume the flat back position.

2. Reach forward with your right leg and lift your toes toward your shin.

3. Relax the knee of your back leg.

4. Repeat on the left.

Rhythmic Arm Reach

1. Extend your left arm.

2. Bend your right arm, keeping your fingers in line with your underarm.

3. Alternate reaching your arms in a rhythmic motion with your shoulders pressed down.

PICTURE THIS	BEWARE!
■ You are moving under water with smooth transitions and controlled positions. ■ Your shoulders, hips, knees, and ankles work as an inflexible unit, all facing the same direction.	■ The warm-up is gradual and gentle. It is not a time for vigorous stretching. ■ Avoid injury by allowing more time to warm up in cooler temperatures.

CHAPTER 10

Chest and Shoulder Muscles

Gymnasts display spectacular feats of **upper-body strength when they compete in Olympic trials.** On the other end of the spectrum, the "I don't know and I don't care" shoulder shrug is not a spectacular feat, but it sure does come in handy.

Your chest muscles, the pectoralis major and minor (pecs for short), are considered a major muscle group. These fan-shaped muscles interact with other muscles, mainly the deltoids, for arm movement and stability.

Pectoral Muscles

Men display their muscled chests as a sign of strength and vitality. Strong chest muscles are primarily associated with hard work—sometimes at the gym. For women, toned chest muscles add contour to the chest, as well as underlying support for the breasts. However, the most compelling reason to develop your pecs is to have increased upper-body strength to live your life with independence and youthful energy.

Your chest muscles, located between your breasts and ribs, connect your chest to your arms. There is no actual muscle in breast tissue, but your underlying pectoral muscles will put up a good front. Corny comments aside, the reality is that after about age forty, your skin becomes more lax (particularly with sun damage), your milk ducts shrink, and your body fat increases. (Other than that, Mrs. Lincoln, how was the play?) Building up your pectoral muscles will add support but won't restore your breasts to their formerly firm, round contours. For that, you need a well-fitting bra or a certified plastic surgeon.

Strong pectoral muscles are desirable—tight ones that pull the shoulder blades, collarbones, and arms forward obviously are not. Most of us engage in activities (such as working at the computer or even cooking) that cause us to hunch forward. Poor posture is also to blame. Continuously being in this position without stretching to open your chest muscles eventually results in consequences such as limited arm movement. Here is an effective stretch you can perform anytime to lengthen your chest muscles. All you need is a doorway.

1. Stand in the middle of an open doorway placing one foot in front of the other.
2. Bend your elbows at right angles and position your forearms on each side of the doorway.
3. Lean forward until you feel a stretch in your chest muscles.
4. Hold for about fifteen seconds while you breathe normally.
5. Relax and repeat several times.

Deltoid Muscles

Broad shoulders have always been a metaphor for physical and emotional strength. Like Atlas, you may have carried the weight of the world on yours. The irony is that the ball-and-socket joints that form your shoulders are also the most unstable and prone to injury. One of the best ways to protect and support your shoulder joints is by strengthening the surrounding muscles—the deltoids and the rotator cuffs.

Your shoulder muscles, or deltoids, form a triangle of three "heads" (front, middle, and rear), which are the most movable joints in your body. They can be used together or separately to move your arms. Your rotator cuffs, which are made up of four muscles and their tendons, stabilize your shoulders and assist in rotation and overhead movements. Athletes who play sports that use overhead motions (such as baseball, softball, swimming, and tennis) benefit from their shoulders' wide range of motion but are plagued by overuse injuries that damage and inflame the muscles and tendons. And you don't have to be an athlete to be vulnerable. Any repetitive movement, such as house painting or window cleaning, can cause rotator cuff fatigue—the best excuse yet for not doing windows.

Toned, nicely rounded shoulders enhance your body's symmetry by being in better balance with your hips. However, the most important reason to develop your deltoid muscles is for the added strength needed to perform everyday tasks, such as carrying a tray if you're a waiter or stowing your carry-on luggage in the plane's overhead compartment when you travel.

It is very important that you maintain all the parts of your shoulders in good working order. Exercising with weights keeps your shoulders strong, and stretching aids in flexibility. A youthful body exudes fluid, flexible movements and toned muscles. Does age rob you of strength and grace? The answer is a resounding no! Your participation in the Body Electric weight-resistance exercises that follow will make all the difference.

Gear

- Use adequate cushioning, such as an exercise mat or a folded towel, between your knees and the floor.
- Use a sturdy chair or bench that won't "skate" on the floor. Anchor it against a wall, if possible.

FYI: You Control the Intensity

You control the intensity of each exercise by varying the weight of your resistance and the speed of your movements. Moving the weights too quickly can be downright dangerous, while there is no downside to working slowly.

Push-Up

Among the following variations, pick the one that you're best able to do and repeat slowly for three and a half minutes or until your form becomes compromised.

BEGINNER

1. Lie chest down on the floor.

2. Bend your elbows and place your hands about shoulder width apart.

3. Bend your knees and position them on the floor, under your hips.

4. Keep your toes on the floor and tucked under.

5. Lower your body with your head positioned between your hands.

6. Slowly straighten both arms to return to the starting position.

INTERMEDIATE or MODIFIED

1. Lie chest down on the floor.

2. Bend your elbows and place your hands on the floor about shoulder width apart.

3. Bend your knees and position them on the floor behind your hips.

4. Lift both feet off the floor.

5. Lower your body with your chest positioned between your hands.

6. Slowly straighten both arms to return to the starting position.

Push-Up, *continued*

ADVANCED

1. Lie chest down on the floor.

2. Bend your elbows and place your hands on the floor about shoulder width apart.

3. Position your straight legs behind your hips.

4. Keep your feet on the floor with your toes tucked under.

5. Lower your body in a straight line with your chin positioned between your hands.

6. Slowly straighten both arms to return to the starting position.

WHAT'S WRONG?

WRONG: The hips are lifted.
RIGHT: The head, back, and hips form a straight line.

VARIATIONS

Hands on Dumbbells

Place your hands on dumbbells rather than the floor if you experience wrist pain in the traditional position.

Modified Push-Up with Bench

Experiment with various bench or chair heights.

Incline Push-Up

Perform modified push-ups in a standing position with your hands on the wall and your feet shoulder width apart and two or three feet away from the wall.

FORM	ANCHORS	PICTURE THIS	BEWARE!
▪ Press your abdomen against your back for support. ▪ Inhale as you bend your arms and exhale as you push up.	▪ Core muscles (abdomen, back, gluteus)	▪ A bobbing duck is moving up and down with its head, neck, and back in a straight line.	▪ Never arch your back.

Dumbbell Fly

1. Lie on your back with your right ankle resting on your bent left knee or with both knees bent.

2. Hold a dumbbell in each hand above your shoulders (your arms basically perpendicular to the floor), with your elbows slightly bent and facing out (your palms facing each other).

3. Lower both arms to about shoulder level (or slightly lower).

4. Lift both arms to the starting position with a slow, steady movement.

VARIATIONS

- **Vary the tempo.** Lower your arms slowly for three counts, and lift on count four. Reverse.
- **Vary the range of motion.** Lift your arms halfway up (only) before lowering to the starting position.

FORM	ANCHORS	PICTURE THIS	BEWARE!
■ Keep your lower back in contact with the floor. ■ Lower your arms keeping your wrists at shoulder level.	■ Chest, lower back	■ Lift your arms as if they are wrapping around a barrel. ■ Lower and lift your arms as a result of your pectoral muscles expanding and contracting.	■ Never lock your elbows.

Stretch

1. Clasp both hands behind your back.

2. Squeeze your shoulder blades toward each other as you reach back.

3. Lift your chest.

DELTOIDS

Side Lateral Raise

Repeat each exercise for three and a half minutes.

1. Holding a dumbbell in each hand, begin with your arms at your sides, palms facing in.

2. Position your feet shoulder width apart.

3. Lift your arms to your sides with your hands about shoulder height.

4. Lower your arms to the starting position.

WHAT'S WRONG?

WRONG: The shoulders and arms are lifting too high.
RIGHT: The shoulders are pressed down, controlling the height that the arms can be lifted.

VARIATIONS

- Lower your arms halfway (only) before lifting.
- Perform the same movements with your palms facing up.

FORM	ANCHORS
▪ Lift your arms only as high as you are able with both shoulders pressed down. ▪ Look in a mirror to keep both shoulders symmetrical. ▪ Keep your wrists fairly straight.	▪ Shoulders, abdomen, gluteus

Dumbbell Press

1. Holding a dumbbell in each hand, bend and lift your elbows to almost shoulder height.

2. Position your wrists approximately over your elbows with your palms facing forward.

3. Extend your arms overhead.

VARIATIONS

- Alternate arms, one down and one up.
- Extend your arms overhead and closer together so that the dumbbells meet in the center.
- Extend your arms overhead and farther apart to form a V.

Rotator Cuff Strengthener

Repeat on each side for three and a half minutes.

1. Lie on your right side with your bottom (right) leg bent at the knee and your top (left) leg extended. Extend your right arm and place it under your head.
2. Holding a dumbbell in your left hand, position your extended arm in front of your chest and shoulder high.
3. Slowly lower and lift your left arm.
4. Repeat while lying on your left side.

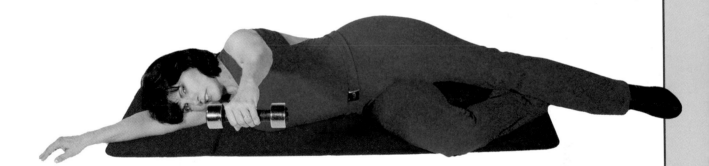

Rotator Cuff Strengthener with Extension

1. Lie on your right side with your bottom (right) leg bent at the knee and your top (left) leg extended.

2. Position your left arm in front of your chest shoulder high, with your elbow bent at 90 degrees and your palm facing your body.

3. Slowly extend your left arm; bend your elbow to return to the starting position.

4. Repeat with your right arm.

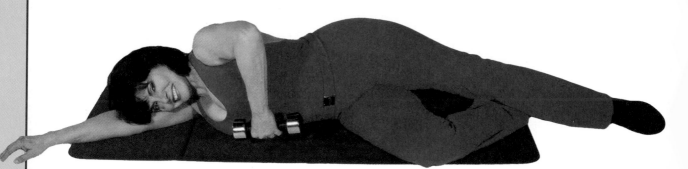

VARIATION

Less difficult

1. Support your left elbow with your right hand.

2. Extend your left arm.

3. Bend your elbow to return to the starting position.

4. Repeat while lying on your left side.

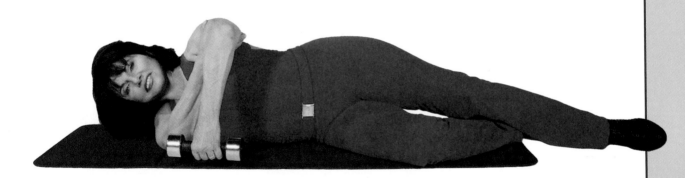

FORM	ANCHORS	PICTURE THIS	BEWARE!
▪ Raise your working arm no higher than your shoulder. ▪ Keep your hips "stacked," one over the other.	▪ Shoulders, abdomen, gluteus	▪ You have weights on your shoulders so that they cannot lift.	▪ Lifting your shoulders will render the exercises less effective and cause tightness in your neck and shoulders.

Stretch

1. Stand with your feet shoulder width apart and grasp your right wrist with your left hand.

2. Gently lengthen your right arm as you tilt your head to the left.

3. Repeat to the right.

CHAPTER 11

The Upper-, Middle-, and Lower-Back Muscles

A sturdy, firm back combined with a shapely waist is synonymous with glamour and beauty. More important, strong back muscles, increased flexibility, and proper body alignment build the foundation for a pain-free back.

Well-conditioned back muscles and ligaments provide support for your spine. Your ligaments hold your bones together, allowing you to perform movements such as bending and twisting within a safe range of motion. Your muscles, like your ligaments, can stretch, plus they have the added ability to contract to coordinate the movement of your bones. And if you need yet another reason to exercise your back muscles, a Mayo Clinic study confirms that stronger back muscles reduce spinal fractures in postmenopausal women.

Increased Flexibility

Stretching is essential for gaining and maintaining flexibility in your spinal column and its surrounding muscles, ligaments, and tendons. Specifically, strong core muscles in your abdomen, gluteus, and lower back allow for flexibility and movement in all directions.

Proper Body Alignment

Research shows that it takes five times more energy to slouch than to stand up tall and straight. When you are off balance, your muscles have to adapt, which can eventually lead to chronic back problems. On the other hand, good posture is stable and energy efficient. With your muscles and bones stacked and balanced, most of your weight is supported and you can move with ease.

Gear

- Always use a well-cushioned exercise mat for variations performed on your hands and knees. Adequate padding allows you to eliminate unnecessary distractions.

FYI: Correct Technique

Correct technique, including moving the weights through a full range of motion, trumps increased resistance every time. If the weights you are using are too heavy to allow you to fully contract your muscles, you can switch to lighter weights or no weights at all. You must always be in complete control of your movements— never compromise correct form or use momentum (swinging movements) to get the job done. A good tip is to use a slow four-second count (one one-thousand, two one-thousand, three one-thousand, four one-thousand) as you lift and lower the weights.

Standing Dumbbell Upright Row

Repeat each exercise for three and a half minutes.

Please note. This compound exercise involves several muscle groups, particularly the trapezius (upper-back muscles) and deltoids. The narrower your grip, the more you will engage the back muscles.

1. Stand with your feet shoulder width apart and hold the dumbbells with an overhand grip (palms facing your body) and your hands fairly close together.

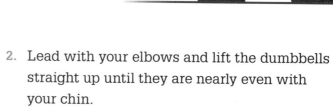

2. Lead with your elbows and lift the dumbbells straight up until they are nearly even with your chin.

3. Slowly return to the starting position.

WHAT'S WRONG?

WRONG: The elbows are not lifted high enough.
RIGHT: The elbows are lifted as high as possible while the shoulders remain pressed down.

WRONG: The arms flare away from the body.
RIGHT: The arms are kept close to the body.

VARIATIONS

- Contract the muscles of your upper back at the top of the movement.
- Perform the movement one arm at a time.

FORM	ANCHORS	PICTURE THIS	BEWARE!
▪ Keep your elbows up and out. ▪ Keep the weights close to your body. ▪ Allow your wrists to flex as you lift the dumbbells.	▪ Shoulders, abdomen, gluteus	▪ Your elbows are leading the movement.	▪ Keep your elbows to the side rather than forward. Lift your elbows, not your shoulders.

Back Dumbbell Row

1. Stand with your feet shoulder width apart and lean forward in the flat back position.

2. Keep your knees slightly bent.

3. Hold the weights straight down (palms facing your body) without locking your elbows.

4. Squeeze your shoulder blades as you lift the weights; extend your arms.

VARIATIONS

- Perform the movement one arm at a time. Rest the nonworking hand on your thigh or a bench.
- Lift the weights with your elbows bent and your wrists positioned under your elbows.

FORM	ANCHORS	PICTURE THIS	BEWARE!
▪ Lift your arms only as high as is possible with your shoulders pressed down. ▪ Maintain your head and neck in alignment with your back. ▪ Expand your chest muscles as you contract your back muscles.	▪ Shoulders, abdomen	▪ The impetus for your arm movement is the contraction and expansion of your upper-back muscles.	▪ Do not squeeze the weights with your hands. Never lock your elbow or knee joints.

Stretch

1. Assume the rounded back position. Place your hands just above your knees.

VARIATION

- Assume the rounded back position and hold a dumbbell in each of your hands to intensify the stretch.

Lower-Back Extension (The Swan)

1. Lie facedown on the floor with your arms at your sides (palms facing your body).

2. Extend your legs behind you.

3. Lift your body off the ground a few inches, keeping your head and neck in alignment.

4. Reach up and back as you raise your arms off the floor.

5. Slowly lower your body and arms back to the floor.

VARIATIONS

- Lie facedown with your hands lightly supporting your head (rather than at your sides).
- **Increase the challenge.** Lift your feet a few inches off the ground as you lift your upper body. Keep your legs straight but not necessarily together. Hold for two to four counts, lower, and repeat.

FORM	ANCHORS	PICTURE THIS	BEWARE!
- Tighten your rear end and lift your abdomen during the entire exercise. - Perform the movements slowly and with control.	- Upper back, abdomen, gluteus	- You are a graceful swan as you lift and lower your torso and arms. - Your body stretches horizontally as it lifts.	- Be careful not to overextend your back as you raise yourself up from your torso. You should feel no more than mild fatigue in your lower back.

Quadruped

1. Begin on your hands and knees, facing the floor with your arms aligned under your shoulders and your knees under your hips.

2. Raise your right arm and left leg off the floor, in line with your body.

3. Hold for ten to fifteen seconds.

4. Lower your right arm and leg to the beginning all-fours position.

5. Repeat with your left arm and right leg.

VARIATIONS

1. Round your back, contract your abdominal muscles, and tuck your chin.

2. Bend your right elbow toward your abdomen.

3. Bend and lift your left leg toward your chest.

4. Return to the extended position.

5. Repeat with your left elbow and right leg.

Less difficult. Extend either your arm or your leg.

FORM	PICTURE THIS	BEWARE!
▪ Tighten your trunk muscles (abdomen and gluteus) for stability. ▪ Maintain a straight line from your head to your tailbone.	▪ You are reaching forward with your extended arm and backward with your extended leg. ▪ Your abdomen is supporting your back.	▪ Do not list, or lean to one side. ▪ Do not allow your extended arm and leg to sink lower than your torso.

Rounded Back Stretch

This is a variation of the yoga-inspired cat stretch.

1. Begin kneeling on all fours, with your knees positioned under your hips and your hands under your shoulders.

2. Tuck your chin in toward your chest.

3. Pull your abdomen against your back.

4. Separate your shoulder blades to open your back (draw your shoulders forward and down).

5. Round your back up and tuck your tailbone down.

CHAPTER 12

Biceps and Triceps

Think of your biceps and triceps as a team (known as antagonistic muscles) that functions to bend and straighten your elbow. When you contract your biceps, your elbow flexes (bends). When you contract your triceps, your elbow extends (straightens). Your elbow is a hinge joint that moves only forward and backward, so it needs just one pair of muscles to make it work.

Your biceps can exert only a pulling force; therefore, the flexed biceps can't be stretched back to their original position without the contraction of the triceps. (The opposite is true when the triceps are contracted.) Understanding this action will help you to recognize the importance of having equal strength in opposing muscles. Avoid injury to your muscles and joints and keep the strength of opposing muscle groups fairly balanced by working your biceps and triceps during a single session.

Gear

- Dumbbells used for weight training are considered a type of free weight. They are relatively inexpensive and are available at most sporting goods and department stores. I recommend that you have on hand several sets in varying weight increments to accommodate exercise variations and levels of intensity. You can combine two dumbbells in the same hand to create more resistance. Simply cross the weights in your hand without involving (weaving) your fingers. Please do *not* improvise with other weighted objects, such as bottles or cans, as they are not ergonomically correct for these movements.

FYI: Correct Breathing

Breathing correctly during exercise will ensure that oxygen is properly transported from your lungs to your muscles. The way you breathe during exercise involves much more than inhaling oxygen and exhaling carbon dioxide. Proper technique maximizes the benefits of every exercise.

Oxygen by itself does not contain usable energy; however, it plays a major role in releasing the energy stored in previously ingested food. The energy demands of your contracting muscles increase during exercise, as does their need for oxygen. Because the air you breathe consists of only 21 percent oxygen, you need to inhale an increased volume of air and oxygen to meet your body's needs. You will know if you are *not* breathing correctly through each repetition because you will be out of breath by the end of the exercise.

To breathe correctly during exercise, do the following:

- Exhale through your mouth in a controlled manner during the most strenuous part of the movement. For example, when you are performing the biceps curl, exhale as you lift your arms to contract your muscles.
- Inhale through your nose during the easier part of the exercise. When working your biceps, inhale as you lengthen your muscles to return to the starting position.
- Be sure there is adequate ventilation during your workout. Excessive yawning can result from a lack of fresh air.

Neeless to say, incorrect breathing is better than holding your breath.

Biceps Curl

Repeat each exercise for three and a half minutes.

1. Stand upright holding a dumbbell in each hand with your palms facing away from your body.

2. Position your feet about shoulder width apart and distribute your weight evenly between both feet.

3. Relax your knees.

4. Press your elbows to your sides.

5. Bend your elbows and lift your arms (keeping your upper arms next to your body) to fully contract your biceps.

6. Lower your arms slowly to fully extend your biceps and return to the starting position.

WHAT'S WRONG?

WRONG: The arms are flared away from the body.
RIGHT: The wrists, elbows, and shoulders are aligned.

VARIATIONS

Repeat each exercise for three and a half minutes.

- Seated version

  1. Sit upright on a sturdy bench or chair with your knees and hips at about the same level.
  2. Hold the dumbbell in your right arm and brace your working arm against your leg.
  3. Bend and lift your arm to contract your biceps.
  4. Slowly lower your arm to fully extend your biceps and return to the starting position.
  5. Repeat with the left arm.

Biceps Curl, continued

- Perform the movements in the standing position with both palms facing various directions: in (facing each other), up, or down.
- Perform the movements with alternating arms, one arm lifting while the other lowers.
- Create varied patterns by changing your range of motion and your tempo. For example, vary the tempo by holding and squeezing your biceps for three counts at the top of the movement (the contraction) before lowering on count four; vary the range of motion by lowering or lifting the weights halfway down or up, respectively, to elbow height.

FORM	PICTURE THIS	BEWARE!
■ Keep your spine in a neutral position, maintaining the natural curve of your back (contrasted with the pelvic tilt, where the lower spine is pressed forward). ■ Tighten your core muscles (abdomen and gluteus) to stabilize your torso. ■ Press your shoulders down and maintain them in a level position. ■ Contract your biceps as much as possible before returning your arm to the extended position. ■ Keep your fingers relaxed at all times. ■ When muscle fatigue prevents you from completing a movement with proper form, it is OK to use your nonworking arm to provide an assist. (Support your working arm by providing a gentle lift with your nonworking arm.)	■ The contraction and expansion of your biceps control your arms' movement. ■ My finger is wedged between your biceps and forearm. Contract your biceps to squeeze my finger as hard as you can. ■ Your chest lifts as your arms lengthen.	■ Do not lock your elbows in the extended position. ■ Locked knees cause strain in your lower back. ■ Do not allow your elbows to flare away from or move behind your body. ■ Do not overly arch your back or lean forward to accommodate increased intensity. ■ The "death grip" (gripping the weights too tightly) causes blood to pool in your extremities. Relax your fingers as much as possible to allow the normal flow of blood. ■ Do not rest your elbow on your leg while in the seated position.

Stretch

1. Stand upright with your feet together and your arms at your sides.

2. Lengthen your working arm as much as possible by using your other arm to press your fingers back and upward.

Triceps Extension

Repeat each exercise for three and a half minutes.

1. Lie on your back on a mat.

2. Bend both knees and position your feet slightly in front of your knees.

3. Extend both arms over your head.

4. Hold one (heavier) dumbbell in your hands with your palms facing up.

5. Without changing your elbow placement, bend your elbows and reach your hands back and down toward the floor to expand your triceps muscles.

VARIATIONS

- Perform the movements with your palms facing each other.

- Perform the movements with your palms facing down.
- Perform the movements positioning the dumbbell over your forehead (rather than behind your head). Your shoulders are positioned under your bent elbows.
- Vary the range of motion and pace. For example, instead of a full extension, lift the weights only as high as your elbows before returning to the starting position. For a change of pace, hold your arms down in the extended position for three counts and lift on count four.

FORM	PICTURE THIS	BEWARE!
▪ Position your elbows close together and facing the ceiling. ▪ Bend your knees to ensure that your lower back is protected (pressed to the floor).	▪ An imaginary bar is positioned beneath your elbows so they cannot lower. ▪ Your elbows are attracted to each other via strong magnets. ▪ Your arms lengthen and contract as a result of your triceps contracting and expanding.	▪ Do not place your hands too close together or allow your elbows to flare out. ▪ Do not lock your elbows during the extension. Never stress your joints to strengthen your muscles. ▪ Do not flex your wrists to perform the action.

Triceps Push-Up

Repeat on each side for three and a half minutes.

1. Lie on your right side with your bottom (right) leg bent at the knee and your top (left) leg extended in line with your top (left) hip.

2 Position your top (left) arm in front of your body with your elbow bent and your hand in line with your bottom (right) shoulder.

3. Wrap your bottom (right) arm around your chest.

4. Lift your upper body in a straight line to contract your triceps.

5. Return to the starting position by leading with your right shoulder as you lower your upper body to the floor.

6. Repeat while lying on your left side.

WHAT'S WRONG?

WRONG: The head, neck, and shoulders are not in alignment.
RIGHT: The head, neck, and shoulders are lowered in one straight line.

VARIATION

- Vary the pace and range of motion. For example, to change the pace, hold in the bent-arm position (triceps expanded) for three counts before extending your arm (contracting your triceps) on the fourth count.

FORM	PICTURE THIS	BEWARE!
▪ Maintain the alignment of your head, neck, and chest as you straighten and bend your top (left) arm to contract and expand your triceps. ▪ Press your shoulders down. ▪ Keep your hips stacked one over the other. ▪ Tighten your core muscles to stabilize your torso.	▪ Your upper body moves as one inflexible unit.	▪ Your supporting (left) hand should be in line with your bottom (right) shoulder. ▪ Do not allow your body to roll forward or backward. ▪ Do not allow your head to drop lower than your shoulders (out of alignment). ▪ Do not allow your feet to lift off the floor.

Stretch

1. Hold a dumbbell vertically in your working hand with your elbow positioned next to and slightly behind your head.

2. Secure your working arm close to your head by holding it with your opposite hand, palm facing down.

3. Allow the weight of the dumbbell to lengthen your triceps.

4. Repeat on the other side by holding the dumbbell in the other hand. (This stretch can be performed without using a dumbbell.)

CHAPTER 13

Abdominal and Oblique Muscles

Your abdominal muscles are actually a group of six muscles that originate on the sternum and ribs and extend to areas of your pelvis. They assist with your movement, breathing process, and posture. Your abdominal muscles shorten and your back muscles lengthen to move your shoulders forward toward your hips. The reverse action creates backward flexion. The muscles that are deeper and closer to your spine contribute the most structural support.

While your abdominal muscles can't be separated (they all work together in each exercise), there are exercises that favor certain portions of the abs. It's helpful to be familiar with your core abdominal muscles so you can target them by picturing them in your mind's eye as you exercise. They are:

- **Transverse abdominus.** Your deepest abdominal muscles are centrally located and wrap around your torso.
- **Internal and external obliques.** Located on the sides and front of your abdomen, these muscles work together to affect your posture as well as the rotation and sideways movement of your spine.
- **Rectus abdominus.** The most superficial of the abdominal muscles, this is a long muscle that extends along the front of your abdomen. Your rectus abdominus can be developed into what are referred to as six-pack abs.

Map Your Strategy

Now that you are familiar with the lay of the land, it's important to dispel a common myth: *you cannot "spot" reduce fat in the abdomen*—or anywhere else, for that matter. If the muscles of your abdomen are smoothed over by a layer of body fat, you have to reduce your body fat overall to whittle your waistline. Body fat responds to diet and aerobic exercise, and you will probably lose body fat most rapidly in the areas of greatest deposit.

Gear

- Lucky you! You were born with all the tools necessary to maintain toned, tight abdominal muscles—no additional gadgets required (although, you may choose to use a small ball and a chair, as suggested for some of the exercises). The muscles in your core area work like any other: you have to expand and contract them through a full range of motion to create fatigue.

FYI: Vary Your Routine

Or more accurately, don't have a set routine. I have included a number of exercise variations for your abdominal muscles because repeating the same exercises over time encourages your body to adapt, thereby reducing the benefits. You will find that some variations are more intense than others—and that's the point. As your muscles increase in tone and strength, you'll welcome the challenge.

Abdominal Crunch

Repeat each exercise for three and a half minutes.

Works the rectus abdominus

1. Lie on a mat on the floor.

2. Place your hands, unclasped, behind your head with your elbows open to the sides.

3. Bend your knees and place your feet flat on the floor, with your ankles forward of your knees.

4. Keep your lower back in constant contact with the floor.

5. Lift your head, neck, and chest in one inflexible line with your chin facing the ceiling.

6. Lower yourself slowly, stopping just before your shoulders touch the floor.

VARIATIONS

- Perform multiple crunches with one leg extended on the floor and repeat using the other leg.

- Perform multiple crunches with your extended leg elevated and your knees side by side (repeat using the other leg).

Abdominal Crunch, *continued*

- Perform crunches with a small ball placed under your upper back.

- Perform crunches with both feet elevated on a bench, chair, or wall.

The Plank

Works the transverse abdominus

1. Begin the exercise on your forearms and knees.

2. Push up until you're resting on your elbows and toes.
3. Keep your back flat, in a fairly straight line from your head to your heels.
4. Maintain the position as long as you are able to do so with correct form (twenty to sixty seconds).
5. Return to the beginning position.
6. Repeat.

The Plank, continued

WHAT'S WRONG?

WRONG: The hips are lifted.
RIGHT: The body forms a straight line from head to heels.

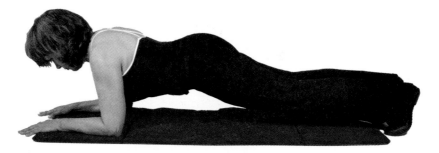

VARIATION

- Lift and hold one leg a few inches off the floor; repeat on the other side.

FORM

- Press your abdomen up to support your back.
- Keep your shoulders and hips square (equal distance) from the floor.
- Position your elbows under your shoulders.

Side Bridge

Works the internal and external obliques

1. Lie on your right side with your bottom (right) knee bent and your top (left) leg extended.

2. Support your upper body with your right elbow positioned directly beneath your right shoulder. Place your left hand behind your head.

3. Tighten your abs and use your torso to lift your hips.

4. Keep your head, neck, and chest in a straight line.

5. Hold this position for ten to fifteen seconds.

6. Lower your hips and repeat on the same side.

7. Repeat on your left side.

Side Bridge, continued

- Lower your left elbow to touch your right hand.
  Raise your elbow back up in line with your shoulder.
  Repeat several times on this side and then repeat
  on the other side.

- **Increase the challenge.** Perform the movements with both legs extended.

FORM

- Contract your gluteals and abdominals to keep your body in correct alignment.
- Be careful not to let your top hip rotate forward.

Bicycle

Works all abdominal muscles

1. Lie on a mat on the floor.

2. Place your hands, unclasped, behind your head with your elbows open to the sides.

3. Bring your knees up to about a 45 degree angle.

4. Slowly curl your upper body diagonally, moving your left shoulder toward your right knee, then your right shoulder to your left knee.

FORM	PICTURE THIS	BEWARE!
• Breathe evenly throughout the exercise. • Lead with your shoulders rather than your elbows. • Keep your head back with your chin facing the ceiling, as much as possible. • Keep your abs contracted throughout the movement to protect your back.	• The weight of the average adult human head is about twelve pounds. (Curious? Lying down with your head on a scale would give you a reasonably close number.) Feel the weight of your head on your hands as you lift and lower. • Your body lifts as a result of your abdominal muscles contracting and lowers as a result of the muscles lengthening.	• Do not pull your head forward to initiate the movement.

Stretch

1. Lie on your back on the floor.

2. Position your knees to one side with your arms overhead and positioned to the opposite side.

3. Try to keep both shoulders on the floor.

Standing Oblique Crunch

Works internal and external obliques

1. Stand with your feet about shoulder width apart and your knees bent.

2. Place your left hand on your left leg, just above your knee.

3. Reach your right arm overhead and to the left.

4. Stretch your right side as you reach up diagonally; "crunch" your rib cage toward your left hip bone. Your hips anchor the movement and remain in place.

5. Bring your right elbow down to meet your right hip as you contract your oblique muscles on your right side.

6. Repeat slowly for about one and a half minutes on one side.

7. Repeat on the other side.

Standing Oblique Crunch, *continued*

WHAT'S WRONG?

WRONG: The knees are straight.
RIGHT: The knees are relaxed to protect the lower back.

WRONG: The arm is reaching too far forward.
RIGHT: The overhead arm is in line with the ear.

VARIATIONS

- Hold a weight in the hand of your lower arm.

- Perform the exercise with your hands on your shoulders.

FORM	PICTURE THIS	BEWARE!
▪ Your extended arm is in line with your ear, palm facing up. ▪ Contract your gluteus to help anchor your hips.	▪ You are reaching up to the exact spot where the ceiling meets the wall.	▪ Do not lift either hip.

Stretch

1. Bend both knees.

2. Place both hands on your legs just above your knees.

3. Lean forward in the flat back position.

4. Straighten your right arm as you lean your right shoulder toward your left knee; repeat on the other side.

CHAPTER 14

Hamstrings and Quadriceps

175

When people talk about hamstrings, they are usually referring to the three separate muscles that stretch from the rear end to the back of the knee. Actually, a hamstring is one of the string-like tendons felt on either side of the back of the knee. Your muscles pull on the tendons to bend your knees and straighten your hips (when you move your leg backward).

Surprisingly, your large hamstring muscles are minimally involved with normal walking and are inactive when you stand, but when you lean forward to sit down or tie your shoes, all three hamstring muscles are engaged. Your hamstrings are extremely important in activities requiring power, such as running, jumping, and climbing, which is usually how most hamstring injuries occur. Athletes exercise with resistance to create stronger, faster leg muscles. The rest of us can also benefit from stronger, faster leg muscles—throw in shapely, and it's a deal you can't refuse.

The muscles of your quadriceps and hamstrings work as a team of antagonists. Because muscles can only exert a pulling force, the contraction of your quadriceps causes your hamstrings to relax, and vice versa. Located on the front of your thigh, your quadriceps tendons attach the four strong quadriceps muscles to your kneecap and extend down to your shin. Your muscle pulls on your tendons to straighten your knee. If you have well-developed quadriceps muscles and your hamstring strength is less than two-thirds the strength of your quadriceps, the imbalance makes you more vulnerable to injury.

Spend time strengthening and stretching your hamstrings and quadriceps. Hamstrings tend to be tight, so it is especially important to stretch them after each workout. Tight hamstrings are often the culprits in lower-back pain by causing your hips and pelvis to rotate back, thereby flattening your lower back. This position stretches the ligaments in your lower back and stresses your disks. Always maintain the natural curve in your lower back whether standing, sitting, or lying down. Never allow your back to flatten or bow out.

If you sit at your desk every day with poor posture, your hamstrings may tighten. Correcting your posture and stretching will do you a world of good.

- **Poor sitting posture.** Your hips slide forward in the chair and your lower back rounds with the tailbone tucked under.
- **Correct sitting posture.** Your back is straight and your shoulders are back. Your rear end touches the back of your chair.

Stretch your hamstrings at your desk, on the plane—wherever, whenever:

1. Use correct sitting posture.
2. Straighten one knee, flex your toes up, and lift your tailbone (similar to the flat back position).
3. Keep your weight evenly distributed on both hips.
4. Hold for about fifteen seconds and repeat on the other side.

Gear

- I recommend that you purchase leg weights to add intensity to the workout. They can be worn around your ankle or above your knee.
- For the standing variation, use a support only for balance. For the sitting variation, choose a chair with a sturdy seat at a height that positions your knees and hips at about the same level. For additional support, place a ball or a small pillow behind your back.

Hamstring Curl

Repeat on each side for three and a half minutes.

1. Begin on all fours with your knees bent directly under your hips and your elbows bent under your shoulders.

2. Straighten your right leg and maintain at hip height, with your toes facing the floor.

3. Bend your right knee and squeeze your heel toward your gluteus to contract your hamstrings.

4. Slowly straighten your right knee to return to the extended position.

5. Repeat with your left leg.

VARIATIONS

Hamstring Extension

1. Extend your right leg.
2. Lift your leg just above hip height.
3. Lower your leg to touch the floor with your toe.
4. Repeat with your left leg.

Curl with Ball

1. Wedge a ball between your calf and hamstrings.
2. Lift your knee to hip height.
3. Lower your knee to the floor (next to your supporting knee).
4. Repeat with the other leg.

- Perform any of the variations in a slow, controlled "pulse" to intensify the muscle contraction.
- Add variety to your workout by establishing a mixed pattern of movements, performing each variation several times before proceeding to the next. Then, repeat the entire pattern.

FORM	PICTURE THIS	BEWARE!
■ Lift your abdomen to support your back. ■ Separate your shoulder blades to open and lift your back. ■ Maintain a fairly straight line from your head to your tailbone (knee and heel). ■ Face the floor squarely (an equal distance from the floor) with both hips and shoulders. Press down on the hip of the working leg.	■ You have a bar beneath your knee that keeps your knee at hip height (when appropriate).	■ Do not lift your working hip. ■ Do not allow your shoulders and hips to slide back into a position behind your elbows and knees. ■ Do not drop your head down so that it is out of alignment with your neck and back.

Bent-Knee Hip Lift

Repeat each side for three and a half minutes.

1. Begin on your back with your left leg bent and your left foot flat on the floor.

2. Wrap your hands under your right knee and press it toward your chest.

3. Raise both hips off the floor and create a "bridge" from your shoulders to the knee of your supporting (left) leg.

4. Lower and repeat slowly with control. You will feel the fatigue in the hamstring of your supporting left leg.

5. Repeat with your right leg bent.

VARIATIONS

- Perform the movement with your right ankle resting on your left knee.

- **Less difficult.** Place your hands on the floor.
- **Increase the challenge.** Cross your arms and place them over your abdomen.
- Perform the movement with your right leg extended over your right hip.

- Rather than repeat the same movement, perform each of the variations eight times before proceeding to the next. Then repeat the entire pattern.

Bent-Knee Hip Lift, continued

VARIATIONS, CONTINUED

- Perform the movement with the supporting (left) leg on a bench, chair, or wall rather than on the floor.

FORM	PICTURE THIS	BEWARE!
■ Square both hips and shoulders to the floor and lift evenly. ■ Place the foot of your bent, supporting leg under, or slightly in front of, your knee. ■ Keep your supporting foot flat on the floor, with your weight on your heel and your toes relaxed. ■ **Less difficult.** Begin with a small range of motion close to the floor. ■ **Increase the challenge.** Lift your hips higher.	■ In the extended up position you have a magnet on the bottom of your foot that is attracted to a magnet on the ceiling.	■ Do not use momentum to hoist your hips up. ■ Do not position your supporting foot behind your knee and close to your hip. ■ Do not place your hands on top of your knee to bring your knee to your chest as this compresses your kneecap.

Standing Hamstring Curl

Repeat each side for three and a half minutes.

1. Stand and place both hands on a chair and square your shoulders, hips, and knees to the chair. Relax the knee of your supporting leg.

2. Place your right toe slightly behind your left heel. Tighten your core muscles (abdomen and gluteus).

Standing
Hamstring Curl, continued

3. Bend your right knee and contract your hamstrings to lift your right foot to about knee height.

4. Lower your foot to return to the starting position.

5. Repeat slowly with control.

6. Repeat with the left leg.

VARIATIONS

- With your knee bent and foot lifted, slowly pulse your heel up and down through a small range of motion before extending your foot back to the floor.
- **Increase the challenge.** Add leg weights.

FORM	BEWARE!
- Tighten your core muscles (abdomen and gluteus) throughout the exercise.	- Do not lean forward onto the chair. - Do not lock the knee of your supporting leg.

Stretch

1. While standing, bend both knees and place your hands just above your knees.

2. Assume the flat back position.

3. Extend one leg forward and flex your toes up toward your shin.

4. Repeat with the other leg.

Quadriceps Leg Extension

Repeat each side for three and a half minutes.

1. Sit on the floor and position your bent elbows on the floor under your shoulders.

2. Place a ball behind your back for support.

3. Maintain proper alignment from your head to your tailbone.

4. Place your left foot on the floor slightly in front of your bent left knee.

5. Extend your right leg just above the floor.

6. Raise your extended leg no higher than the knee of your supporting leg.

7. Lower to the beginning position.

8. Repeat with the left leg.

Knees Side by Side

1. Sit on the floor with a ball behind your back for support and bend both knees side by side.

2. Extend your right leg.

3. Bend your right knee and lower your foot.

4. Tap the floor with your toe (only) before extending your leg again.

5. Repeat with the left leg.

In a Chair

1. Perform the leg extension while seated in a chair.

FORM	BEWARE!
■ Keep your shoulders down and your chest lifted.	■ Do not use momentum to lift your leg.
■ If you feel discomfort in your hip flexors, change the angle of your leg.	■ Do not sink into your shoulders.

Stretch

1. Lie on the floor on your right side.

2. Bend both knees forward with your knees and feet stacked one over the other.

3. Reach behind to hold your left ankle with your hand.

4. Stretch to lengthen the area from your hip to your knee.

5. Lie on your left side and repeat.

Quadriceps Lunge with Dumbbells

Repeat each side for three and a half minutes.

1. Stand and place one foot on the floor in front of the other.
2. Hold the dumbbells down at your sides.
3. Square your shoulders, hips, and knees to face the same direction.
4. Bend both knees, maintaining a straight line from your head to your back knee.
5. Position your bent front knee over your front ankle.
6. Position your bent back knee under your hip.
7. Lift your back heel off the floor as you bend and straighten both knees.
8. Repeat with the other foot in front.

Quadriceps Lunge with Dumbbells, continued

WHAT'S WRONG?

WRONG: The front (left) knee is forward of the left ankle.
RIGHT: The front knee is positioned directly over the front ankle, thereby placing less stress on the knee.

WRONG: The shoulders and hips are not square. The left side is pulled farther back than the right side and the shoulders are not level.
RIGHT: The shoulders and hips are kept in alignment.

VARIATIONS

- Begin with a full range of motion, and progress to a partial range of motion, lifting your body only halfway up before repeating the lunge.
- **Less difficult.** Perform the exercise without dumbbells. Place both hands above the knee of your front leg.

BEWARE!

- Do not allow your front knee to move forward of your front ankle.
- If this happens, shift your body back so that your shoulders are centered over your hips and back knee.
- Your weight should be on your back foot.

Stretch

1. Stand and maintain your balance with or without additional support.

2. Position your ankles and knees side by side.

3. Bend your left knee and reach back to bring your left heel up toward your gluteus.

4. Keep your knees side by side as you lengthen your quadriceps muscles from your hip to your knee.

5. Repeat standing on your left foot.

CHAPTER 15

Inner and Outer Thighs

Be glad you're not an octopus. Imagine having to exercise all of those inner and outer thighs! If you're like most women, you probably have invested more than enough energy in the two you have—which usually take the rap when a few extra pounds cause your jeans to feel snug. How many times have you looked at your body critically rather than accepting or even admiring it? We women of the baby boomer generation ushered in the exercise revolution, so it stands to reason that we want to continue looking good in our jeans. Most important, we want to exude health and vitality.

As you know by now, your genetics play a major role in the shape and composition of your body. If your body is pear shaped—rather than the more round apple shape—you have the classic hourglass figure with a small waist and wider shoulders and hips. You tend to carry your excess body weight in your lower torso: thighs, hips, abdomen, rear end, and knees. It's a good bet that your mom and Aunt Mary share a similar body type; however, it is what you do with your inherited traits that makes all the difference.

Your inner thighs, called hip adductors, are strips of muscle that run from your pelvic area to your inner thighbone and move your leg toward and across your body's midline. The adductors stabilize and coordinate the movements of your legs and pelvis as you stand, walk, lunge, and climb. They are somewhat harder to target with resistance-type exercise; however, it is important to create balance between opposing muscle groups (inner and outer thighs).

Your outer thighs, called hip abductors, are strips of muscle that attach at the top of your pelvis and the top of your thighbone and move your leg away from your body. The abductors give shape to your upper hips. Your outer thighs need ample strength to stabilize your pelvis when you walk and to help your quadriceps stabilize your knee joint so you can balance on one leg.

I had a reality check recently when I received a message from a "Body Electric" viewer regarding the exercises that require the inner thighs to press together. The message read, "Honey, my thighs are always touching!" You will find that aerobic exercise and diet are the most effective weapons for reducing the collections of body fat in your thigh area—fancy terms for this fat include *saddlebags* and *cellulite*. Additionally, there is also great benefit in drinking more plain water. When your body is amply hydrated, you have less water retention, which helps reduce the appearance of saddlebags and cellulite.

The muscle-toning exercises that follow are intended to shape and strengthen the muscles of your inner and outer thighs.

Gear

- The ball is a perfect complement to the inner-thigh exercises. For the inner-thigh lifts on the floor, the ball provides a comfortable prop to support your nonworking leg and keep your knee in alignment with your hips. For the inner-thigh squeeze, it is the perfect tool to create resistance for your inner thighs and the perfect size that allows alignment of your hips, knees, and ankles.

FYI: Pay Attention to "the Shakes"

If you feel trembling in your muscles during your workout, the sensation usually lasts only a short time and generally subsides quickly after you have rested your muscles. Possible causes include:

- Your muscles are being stretched too vigorously.
- Your muscles are overly fatigued.
- Your muscles are trying to exert control over unfamiliar movements.
- You are lacking proper nutrition or hydration.

Inner-Thigh Lift

Repeat each side for three and a half minutes.

1. Lie on your right side and rest your head on your extended right arm.

2. Create a straight line from your head to your tailbone. Square and align your hips and shoulders, one over the other (also known as "stacking" your hips and shoulders).

3. Reach forward with your top arm to open your back and keep your shoulders and hips from rolling backward.

4. Extend your lower leg in line with your lower hip.

5. Bend your top leg at a right angle (think L shape for "leg") with your knee in front of your hip, supported by the ball, and your ankle in line with your knee.

6. Exhale as you slowly lift your lower leg through a full range of motion. Hover at the top of the movement.

7. Slowly lower your leg to the starting position.

8. Repeat lying on your left side.

VARIATIONS

Less difficult
- Bend the knee of your working leg as working a longer lever is more difficult.

Increase the challenge
- Add leg weights.
- Draw small circles with your extended leg, both clockwise and counterclockwise, before lowering.
- Shorten the range of motion by lifting your leg to the top of the range and lowering only halfway.
- Hold your leg at the top of the range for three counts and lower it on the fourth.

FORM	PICTURE THIS	BEWARE!
- Keep your hips stacked one over the other. Engage your abdominal muscles to help stabilize your spine and pelvis.	- The muscles of your inner thigh are initiating the action by pulling your leg up and then pushing your leg down.	- Do not allow your shoulders and hips to roll back.
- Keep both knees facing forward.		- Do not let the foot of your working leg hang limply. Maintain a straight line from your hip to the tip of your toes.
- Intensify the muscle contraction by pressing down against the ball with your bent upper leg as you press up with your working leg.		
- If your top leg feels uncomfortable at a right angle, move your knee to create a lesser angle. Keep your ankle positioned under your knee.		

Inner-Thigh Ball Squeeze

1. Sit in a sturdy chair that positions your knees directly in front of and level with your hips.

2. Place your ankles under your knees.

3. Place the ball between your knees.

4. Squeeze the ball and then release with your inner thighs and knees using slow, controlled movements.

VARIATIONS

- Perform the exercise on your back with your feet on a bench, chair, or wall. Position your knees over your hips and your feet in line with your knees.
- Perform the exercise in a standing position.
- **Increase the challenge.** Squeeze for three counts and release on the fourth.

FORM	BEWARE!
▪ The squeeze is more of a hold than a bouncing movement.	▪ Do not fully release the ball between contractions, as that will decrease the intensity.
▪ Sit tall in your chair and maintain the natural curve of your lower back. (*Optional:* place a pillow behind your lower back for added support.)	
▪ Keep your feet flat on the floor.	

Stretch

Stretch your inner thighs one at a time. You will feel a gentle stretch in the inner thigh of your extended leg.

1. Sit on the floor placing equal weight on both hips.

2. Extend your right leg and bend your left.

3. Lean forward with a flat back.

4. Place your fingertips in front of you on the floor and "walk" them forward to increase forward flexion of your hips.

5. Maintain proper body alignment—don't round your back.

6. Repeat with your left leg extended.

OUTER THIGHS

Outer-Thigh Lift

Repeat each side for three and a half minutes.

1. Lie on your right side with the ball supporting your rib cage.

2. Reach forward with your top (left) arm to open your back and keep your shoulders and hips from rolling backward.

3. Bend your knees forward of your body.

4. Stack your knees and ankles, one over the other.

5. Lift your top (left) leg no higher than your hip.

6. Slowly lower your top leg until it barely touches your bottom leg.

7. Repeat lying on your left side.

Outer-Thigh Lift, continued

VARIATIONS

- Perform the exercise lying on the floor without the ball for support and your head resting on your right arm.

- **Increase the challenge.** Perform the exercise with your top (left) leg fully extended.

- Vary the range of motion, lowering your leg only halfway.
- Vary the pace by holding your leg at the top of the movement for three counts before lowering it.
- Intermix the movements in various combinations.

WHAT'S WRONG?

WRONG: The knee of the top (left) leg is facing up.
RIGHT: The knee is facing forward in line
with the hip and foot.

FORM	PICTURE THIS	BEWARE!
▪ Square and align your hips and shoulders, one over the other.	▪ The air is thick (like soup) and you have to exert pressure to lift and lower your leg.	▪ Do not allow your shoulders and hips to roll back.
▪ Exhale as you slowly lift your upper leg through a full range of motion. Hover at the top of the movement.		▪ Do not let the foot of your working leg hang limply.
▪ Lift your knee and foot together and on the same plane (level). (If you look at your knee, you should not be able to see your foot.)		▪ Do not lead the movement with your knee facing up.
▪ Both of your knees face forward throughout the exercise.		▪ Do not lean on the ball. Use it only as a support for your rib cage.
▪ **Less difficult.** Do not use leg weights, or place the leg weight above your knee rather than on your ankle.		
▪ **Increase the challenge.** Create more intensity by performing the exercise using both leg weights on one leg (place one leg weight above your knee and the other on your ankle).		

Standing Outer-Thigh Lift

Repeat each side for three and a half minutes.

1. Using a chair or other support for balance, stand with your feet together and "square" your shoulders, hips, knees, and feet to face the same direction.

2. Center your weight over your supporting (left) leg.

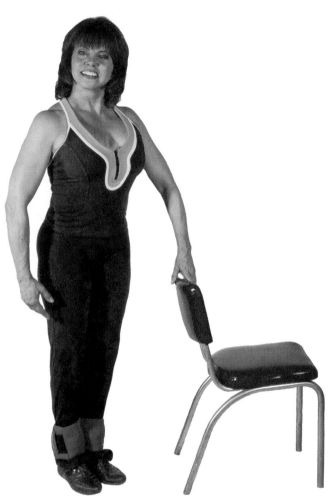

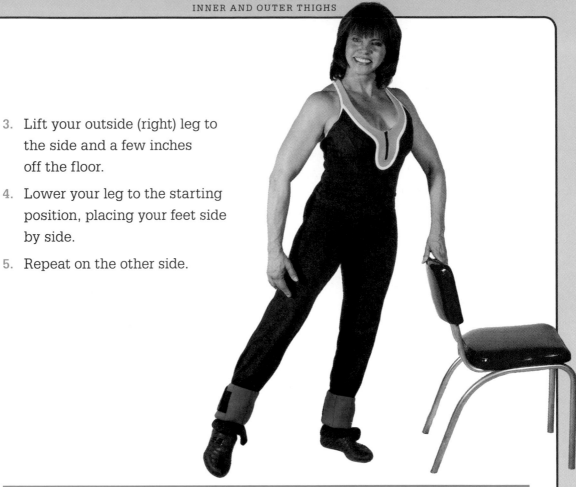

3. Lift your outside (right) leg to the side and a few inches off the floor.

4. Lower your leg to the starting position, placing your feet side by side.

5. Repeat on the other side.

VARIATIONS

- Vary the range of motion and the pace.
- **Less difficult.** Perform the exercise with no ankle weights.
- Draw circles just above the floor with your extended leg.

FORM	BEWARE!
■ Tighten your core muscles (abdomen and gluteus) to stabilize your torso.	■ Do not lean on the chair. (Use one finger for balance.) Maintain correct alignment from your head to your tailbone.
■ To improve your alignment, face the back of the chair squarely and place both hands on the chair.	■ Do not use a support that is too high and causes your shoulders to lift.
■ Lead the movement with your outer thigh rather than your knee.	■ Do not lock your elbows or knees.
■ Relax (slightly flex) the knee of your supporting leg.	

Stretch

1. Lie on your back on the floor.

2. Bend both legs and position your knees over your hips.

3. Press your lower back and hips to the floor.

4. Cross your right ankle over your left knee.

5. Wrap both arms around your left thigh.

6. Using your arms, gently press both legs toward your chest.
   You will feel a stretch in the outer thigh of your top (right) leg.

7. Repeat with your left ankle crossed over your right knee.

CHAPTER 16

The Gluteus Muscles

Rear end, caboose, derriere, buttocks—whatever you call yours, you want it to be round, firm, and definitely not in the process of sliding south. I have a theory about rear ends: they don't drop quietly. Rather, they fall like a rock and make a resounding thud that is heard 'round the world. But seriously, the muscles of your gluteus are very resilient. Within a few sessions of performing the gluteus squeeze exercises that follow, you will begin to see a "slider" reverse direction.

The gluteal muscles that make up the human buttocks are actually three muscles: your uppermost gluteus maximus is the largest, with the gluteus minimus and gluteus medius located directly beneath. Your gluteus maximus, one of your body's most powerful muscles, connects your pelvis to the rear of your thighbone, or femur (your other gluteus muscles attach to the sides of your femur). Its most powerful action is to regain your body's erect posture after stooping, by moving your thigh to the rear and drawing your pelvis backward. Understandably, it is the main muscle used by athletes in many sports, such as basketball, football, and volleyball.

Your gluteus maximus is most responsible for the shape and appearance of your rear end, a uniquely human feature. The other major contributing factor is adipose tissue, more commonly known as body fat, which gives your rear end its rounded shape—or, less desirably, its saggy appearance. While the size and shape of your rear end is a major cosmetic consideration, your more significant concern should be its functionality. Perhaps your lower back hurts or you are slower to get up from a chair or to climb stairs as the result of inactivity, which has caused your gluteal muscles to atrophy.

Let's put an end (guilty as charged of extreme corniness) to gluteal muscles that have become slow and weak. A muscular, perky rear end not only looks better, but it supports energetic movement, increased vigor, and weight loss. Bottom line: a stronger, more functional gluteus is also a shapelier one.

Gear

○ Use leg weights over your hips to provide more comfortable resistance. You can also use a dumbbell over a folded towel or by itself.

FYI: Increased Intensity for Maximum Results

To derive the greatest benefits from this or any other exercise requires focus and intensity. Add resistance when you are able, and be sure that you contract your gluteal muscles to the max each and every time you squeeze.

The gluteal squeeze variations that follow are totally effective on many levels:

- to shape and strengthen your gluteal muscles
- to restore muscle tone and strength to your pelvic floor (similar to the Kegel exercise)
- to provide therapeutic stretching for your lower back

Gluteal Squeeze

Repeat each exercise for three and a half minutes.

1. Lie on your back on the floor.
2. Position your feet together, flat on the floor and slightly in front of your knees (a safe angle for your knees).
3. Tilt your pelvis up, using your lower back as an anchor.
4. Lead the movement with your tailbone.
5. Curve your vertebrae slowly up and down.
6. Use a small range of motion to squeeze and partially release your gluteal muscles.
7. End the movement with the lowering of your tailbone.

VARIATIONS

- Perform the movement with your heels on the floor and your toes elevated on dumbbells.

- Perform the movement with your feet elevated on a bench, chair, or wall. Position your knees approximately over your hips.

- Vary your leg and foot position as you contract and relax your gluteus muscles: knees and feet shoulder width apart; knees together and feet apart; feet together and knees apart.
- Change the pattern by moving your knees horizontally (in and out) while your feet remain stationary.
- Vary your pace and range of motion. For example, intensify the contraction by holding and squeezing at the top of the range of movement for three counts and partially lowering on the fourth count.

Gluteal Squeeze, continued

WHAT'S WRONG?

WRONG: The hips and back are lifted too high, the arms are on the floor, and the ankles are positioned under the knees.

RIGHT: The abdomen is pressed against the back and the pelvis is tilted up, the arms are folded over the abdomen, and the feet are positioned forward of the knees.

FORM	PICTURE THIS	BEWARE!
■ Maintain a fairly straight line from your head to your tailbone. ■ Place your weight on your heels, and relax your toes while keeping your feet flat on the floor. ■ Lower your hips to a position just above the floor. ■ Relax your upper body. ■ When adding resistance, place it over your hips rather than your abdomen.	■ Like a fist, your gluteal muscles contract in all directions.	■ Do not arch your back during the lifting phase of the movement. ■ Do not place your hands on the floor for added leverage. ■ When your feet are on the floor, do not position your ankles under your knees or close to your hips.

Stretch

1. Lie on your back, bend both knees, and wrap your arms around your thighs and under your knees. (Pressing your arms *over* your knees compresses your kneecaps.)

2. Keep your lower back and tailbone in contact with the floor.

3. Press your knees to your chest.

CHAPTER 17
Calf Muscles

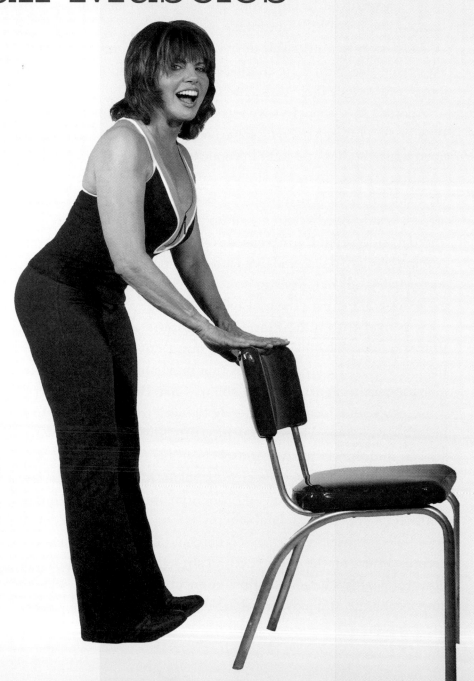

I f you have seen a Riverdance performance, you have surely marveled at the rapid step dancing and the dancers' strong, well-developed calves. And if you are a hiker, you probably have developed your calves as a result of flexing your ankles to navigate the uneven terrain of hills and rocks.

Most significantly, well-developed calf muscles boost your leg power and, with your quadriceps, help to support your knee joints and reduce their wear and tear.

Another plus: shapely, sexy legs are more appealing to the eye. Have you ever wondered why some bodybuilders have overly developed upper bodies and out-of-proportion small legs? It's because building strong, diamond-shaped calf muscles is a difficult but far from impossible training feat. Because your leg muscles are already conditioned to carry your body weight, increased strength and definition require increased resistance. Furthermore, your calf muscles are dense and can withstand more frequent training, so regardless of how your calves are presently shaped, effective exercises will increase the tone and strength of your calves.

It is useful to understand the anatomy of your calves so that you can picture them in your mind's eye as you perform the exercises. The large muscles that make up your calves—the gastrocnemius (gastroc) and soleus—are the most powerful muscles in your lower leg. They both work to extend your foot and flex your toes when you walk, run, jump, or bicycle. Your shorter and thicker gastroc muscle is visible from the outside of your body and raises your heel. Your soleus muscle is positioned under your gastrocnemius and functions in a slightly different manner: it raises your heel when your knee is bent. Because your soleus muscle makes up 60 percent of your calf, it has the greatest effect on the calf's size and strength. Your Achilles tendon, your body's largest tendon, connects your calf muscles to your heel bone and aids in ankle flexion.

Gear

- A sturdy chair with a back that is no higher than the height of your elbows can be used to assist with balance when performing the standing exercises; it can also support correct form when performing the seated variations.
- A block or "step" placed under the toes provides for greater range of motion when lifting and lowering your heels.
- The addition of dumbbells or leg weights increases the intensity of any exercise.

FYI: Cramps Are a Pain in the Muscles

No one is immune to muscle cramps, which are very common. They are an involuntary contraction of a muscle that doesn't relax—and it is never a welcomed experience. Actually, cramps can occur in any skeletal muscle but most commonly occur in your legs, your feet, and the muscles that cross two joints such as the calves. Cramps can affect an entire muscle group or part of a muscle group and can range in intensity from a slight twitch to a severe pain. A cramped muscle can last from a few seconds to a few minutes and keep returning for a period of time, like the aftershocks that follow an earthquake. Fortunately, most muscle cramps are not severe, frequent, or serious.

The exact cause of muscle cramps is unknown; however, most experts agree that they are related to poor flexibility or muscle fatigue or result from performing an unfamiliar movement. They usually go away on their own but never fast enough. Here are some things you can do in the meantime:

- Stop the activity that is causing the cramp—like you have a choice!
- Gently stretch and massage the cramped muscle.
- Remove constricting garments, such as shoes and socks.

Improved fitness, adequate intake of fluid, and stretching of your leg muscles are the best strategies for preventing muscle cramps.

Standing Calf Raise

Repeat each exercise for three and a half minutes.

Works the gastrocnemius

1. Stand tall with your body squarely facing the back of a chair.
2. Position your feet parallel and fairly close together.
3. Place your fingertips on the chair for balance.
4. Contract your calf muscles by slowly lifting your heels through a full range of motion.
5. Lower your heels to the starting position.

- **Increase the challenge.** Position your nonworking (right) foot above the heel of your supporting (left) leg. Contract the calf muscle of your left leg by lifting your left heel as high as possible through a full range of motion.

- Perform the movement with the ball wedged between your knees.

Standing Calf Raise, continued

- Rock back and forth alternating the heel of one foot and the toe of the other. Be sure to complete each movement through a full range of motion.

- Alternately rock back on both heels and then rock forward on all toes.

WHAT'S WRONG?

WRONG: You lean on the chair.
RIGHT: Stand with your body erect and your hands lightly touching the chair for balance.

VARIATIONS

- Add ankle weights.
- When performing the standing one-legged calf raise, hold a dumbbell on the same side as the working leg (use the other hand for support).
- Perform the standing movement on a block or step that is approximately two inches off the ground. Place just the balls of your feet on the block. Hang your heels and arches off the back of the block and initiate the movement from your ankle joint. Slowly lower your heels so they touch the floor and your calf muscles stretch; slowly raise your heels until you are standing on your toes.

"Donkey" Calf Raise

Works the gastrocnemius

1. Stand on a block or step facing a chair.

2. Bend your body forward from your hips at a right angle with your torso parallel to the floor.

3. Place your arms on the chair for support.

4. Keep your knees relaxed but straight.

5. Raise your heels, extending as high as possible.

6. Lower your heels until your calves are being stretched.

7. Your gastrocnemius muscle responds more effectively to a slightly faster tempo and more resistance (add ankle weights). Remember: "gastro go."

FORM	PICTURE THIS	BEWARE!
▪ Tighten your core muscles (abdomen and gluteus) to stabilize your torso. ▪ Place equal weight on all of your toes. ▪ Keep your shoulders down at all times. ▪ Square your shoulders, hips, and knees whether you are facing the chair or away from it.	▪ Use slow, continuous movement (the downward movement of your heel initiates the upward movement). ▪ Your heels are being lifted and lowered by the contraction and expansion of your calf muscles.	▪ Do not lean on the chair with your body out of alignment. ▪ Do not use momentum to perform the movements. ▪ Do not lock your knees.

Seated Calf Raise

Works the soleus

1. Sit forward in a chair and bend your knees at a right angle.

2. Place the dumbbells over your knees. For additional comfort, place a folded towel between the dumbbells and your legs.

3. Work this muscle by slowly lifting your heels, being sure to take each movement through its full range of motion (remember: "soleus slow").

Stretch

1. Sit in a chair with both knees bent at a right angle.

2. Maintain equal weight on both hips.

3. Lean forward in the flat back position.

4. Place your left arm on your left leg.

5. Reach forward with your right arm to stretch the calf of your right leg.

6. Place your hand behind your toes and apply gentle upward pressure.

7. Repeat with your other leg.

CHAPTER 18
The Cooldown

I conclude every workout with a graceful cooldown that moves my body and inspires my soul. For me, grace expresses balance, passion, beauty, strength, humility, and gratitude. It is at once quiet and bold, soothing and stimulating.

Our bodies strive to create balance between strong muscles and flexible joints. The cooldown at the end of each workout gives your body an opportunity to slow down gradually. Following an aerobic activity that elevates your respiration, allow your heart rate and breathing to return to their normal resting rate before you perform the cooldown stretches. (When vigorous activity is stopped abruptly, fainting or dizziness can be caused by blood pooling in the large muscles of your legs.) The exercises in this program challenge your muscles to create strength and definition, and the cooldown exercises are vital for preventing injury.

The goals of the cooldown are as follows:

- Aid in ridding the body of a buildup of waste products, including lactic acid.
- Provide healing oxygen and nutrients needed to repair muscles, tendons, and ligaments by recirculating the blood back to the heart, muscles, and brain. After exercise, the elevated blood pressure that has been pushing blood and waste products back to the heart slows. The resulting pooling of blood in the muscles causes pain and swelling.
- Provide a perfect opportunity to stretch warm muscles and joints for a greater range of motion.

Gear

- Use a towel or a belt to increase your reach.

FYI: Stretching Is for Flexibility and Relaxation

Stretching should be gentle and never painful. Decrease the intensity of a particular stretch if you experience shakiness in your limbs.

Please note. Stretch each muscle group for twenty to thirty seconds using static movements (no bouncing).

Full-Body Stretch

1. Lie on your back and stretch your entire body, creating as long a line as possible, from your fingertips to your toes. Because your legs are fully extended, allow your lower back to arch slightly.

Lower-Back Stretch

BOTH KNEES TO CHEST

1. Lie on your back, bend your knees, and wrap both arms around your thighs, placing your arms *under* your knees.

2. Gently press both knees to your chest.

3. Keep your lower back, hips, and tailbone on the floor.

4. Gently rock your body from side to side.

ONE KNEE TO CHEST

1. Lie on your back, bend your left knee, and wrap both arms around your left thigh, placing your hands *under* your knee.

2. Extend your right leg.

3. Gently press your left knee to your chest.

4. Keep both hips on the floor.

5. Repeat with your right leg.

Hamstring Stretch

1. Lie on your back and bend your right knee, positioning your foot in front of your knee.

2. Keep both hips on the floor.

3. Extend your left leg up with the knee relaxed.

4. Place both hands on your ankle (or knee) and gently stretch your leg toward your chest and head.

5. Repeat with your right leg.

Hamstring Stretch with Towel

- Do the stretch as just described using a towel wrapped around the ball of your foot to extend your reach.

Spine Twist

1. Lie on the floor.

2. Extend your right leg.

3. Bend your left leg and cross it over your right knee.

4. Using your right hand, gently coax your left knee toward the floor.

5. Twist your head and spine back to the left and extend your left arm to the side.

6. Keep both shoulders on the floor.

7. Switch sides.

Lunge Stretch for the Hip Flexors

1. Square your shoulders and hips to face the same direction.

2. Rest your back knee on the floor in the lunge position.

3. Bend your front leg and position your front knee and foot at an approximate right angle.

4. Press your abdomen against your back.

5. Place your hands on your front leg just above your knee.

6. Gently press forward until you feel a stretch in the front of your left hip.

7. Switch legs.

Side Stretch

1. Sit squarely on both hips. (Place a pillow or folded towel under your hips to give you a greater range of motion.)

2. Extend your left leg and place your left arm in front, palm up.

3. Bend your right knee and center your foot in front of your body.

4. Reach up and somewhat over your head with your right arm, palm facing up.

5. Reverse to stretch the other side.

Calf Stretch

1. Sit squarely on both hips. (Place a pillow or folded towel under your hips to give you a greater range of motion.)

2. Extend your left leg.

3. Square both shoulders to face your extended left leg.

4. Reach forward with a flat back and place both hands behind your toes.

5. Gently pull your toes toward your body and press the calf of your extended leg to the floor.

6. Reverse to stretch the other side.

Calf Stretch, continued

Calf Stretch with Towel

- Perform the stretch as just described using a towel wrapped around the ball of your foot to extend your reach.

WHAT'S WRONG

WRONG: The back is rounded.
RIGHT: Create a straight line from your head to your tailbone for correct alignment.

Forward Stretch with Rounded Back

1. Sit on the floor and cross your legs.

2. Separate your shoulder blades to "open" your back.

3. Rest your forearms on the floor, one on top of the other.

4. Bring your head forward to rest on your arms.

5. Slowly lift your spine, head last, to return to the starting position.

Neck Stretch

1. Sit on the floor and cross your legs.

2. Press your left hand to the floor.

3. Using your right hand, tilt your head so your right ear points toward your right shoulder.

4. Repeat to the left.

Overhead Stretch

1. Sit on the floor and cross your legs.

2. Inhale through your nose as you extend your arms overhead. Do not lift your shoulders.

3. Exhale through your mouth as you lower your arms to return to the starting position.

Index